ML

BLANC VITE

Also by Raymond Blanc

RECIPES FROM LE MANOIR AUX QUAT' SAISONS

COOKING FOR FRIENDS

BLANC MANGE

A BLANC CHRISTMAS

BLANC VITE

FAST, FRESH FOOD FROM
RAYMOND BLANC

NUTRITION BY DR JEAN MONRO

HEADLINE

First published in 1998
by HEADLINE BOOK PUBLISHING

First published in softback in 2000
by HEADLINE BOOK PUBLISHING

10 9 8 7 6 5 4 3 2 1

0 7472 7755 9

Edited by Susan Fleming
Designed by the Senate
Photographs by Peter Knab
Food for photography by Alex MacKay
Typeset by Letterpart

Printed and bound in Great Britain by
Butler & Tanner Ltd, Frome and London

HEADLINE BOOK PUBLISHING
A division of the Hodder Headline Group
338 Euston Road
London NW1 3BH

www.headline.co.uk
www.hodderheadline.com

Contents

ACKNOWLEDGEMENTS

I would like to thank a number of people, as well as organisations, for their assistance in the preparation of this book.

Alex MacKay (above), Director of Le Manoir Ecole de Cuisine, gave me tremendous help on a day-to-day basis. Thank you, Alex, for your unfailing support through a very demanding time.

I am indebted to Jean Monro who guided me through the complexity of nutrition. Her knowledge and insight have been invaluable in the writing of this book. My thanks to Susan Fleming, my editor, as well as to the photographic team of Peter Knab, Di Knab and Laurie Bartley for their complete involvement in putting this book together. My gratitude to Corrina Thorne and Elena Giacomelli for their secretarial support.

I would like to thank as well our suppliers Villeroy & Boch, AEG, Meyer UK Ltd, ALNO, Antoine and Tony from Valimex, the Newitt family (our local butcher) and Bobby from Daily Fish.

INTRODUCTION

RAYMOND BLANC

'Let food be your medicine and medicine be your food.'
Hippocrates

Why the above truth, dating from the fifth century BC, has been ignored on the whole by our society, I do not know. However, twenty years in the professional kitchen and twenty before, learning at my mother's side, have taught me that a good life – which means love, clear thinking, harmony and health – starts with good and healthy food. Thus I have written this book containing some 200 simple recipes created following certain elementary nutritional guidelines, which will give you a good understanding of balanced nutrition.

For years nutrition has been regarded as the hobby-horse of self-denying cranks. No wonder. Researching this book, I was confronted on more than one occasion with many contradictions and much misinformation. Typically, in one meeting with five 'nutritionists', I was ordered never to eat spinach ('it's full of dangerous toxins') or pork (an act tantamount to 'cannibalism'), and to ensure that 80 per cent of my diet was carbohydrate. I made my excuses and left with my head reeling.

Such negativity is dangerous, as it makes us totally paranoid about the food we eat. The true principles of nutrition, the intimate secrets that marry food, body and mind, have always enthralled me. Brillat-Savarin, the great early nineteenth-century gastronome, declared, 'Tell me what you eat, and I shall tell you what you are' – in essence, 'You are what you eat.' I smiled with approval and a certain smugness at this, but with no real understanding, as I thought I recognised the classic French, gourmand attitude, 'Oh my little belly, all I earn is for you.' Of course I, of all people, could not entirely deny this passion, but Brillat-Savarin's words apply to us all, expressing something deep, necessary and true. I began to realise this the moment I first touched a frying pan, and knew I had to create flavour, but flavour that was allied with lightness. That somebody must suffer a *crise de foie* or fall off his chair as testimony of a great meal is barbaric.

I am well aware that books concerning nutrition are rarely bestsellers; they are not user-friendly and tend to be entrenched in dogma, with faddy rules and lots of Dos and Don'ts. Before attempting many of their recipes the reader must take a solemn vow of abstinence and prepare himself for a ten-day pilgrimage to specialist shops in order to gather a veritable pharmacy of ingredients. There must be no fat, no meat, no wine, no flavour – and no fun.

This is not the case here, however. Under the guidance of Jean Monro, an eminent doctor in her field, I have explored the parameters of a way of eating that is balanced, that encompasses all foods (limiting only a few), and that delivers flavour, health, satisfaction and, above all, pleasure.

IN THE BEGINNING

Good food starts with wholesome ingredients. Yet we remain complacent. Agriculture has become agrochemistry and, in order to get large yields, we have intensive farming that involves a large spectrum of chemicals damaging both to nature and to ourselves at the end of the food chain.

I witnessed this myself with great clarity, not so long ago. Visiting friends, my hostess, Mrs Drennan, took me outside to see her prized roses. In the previous few days the wind had been gently blowing over from a neighbouring cornfield rich in chemical treatments. Rows and rows of blooms greeted me, all shrivelled or dying.

Despite the work of many enthusiastic proponents of natural farming methods (see the Appendices), Great Britain remains far behind most other European countries in promoting sympathetic agricultural systems, and in ensuring that crops and animals are grown and reared organically. And this, when we can all attest to the indisputable fact that organic meat, eggs, poultry, vegetables and fruit just taste so much better.

To make things worse, food is also now processed in order to make it 'completely safe' and attractive, with a 'healthy look', hence removing every single bacterium and germ; through this we are weakening our natural immunity, which is partly why so many people have allergies today. The food industry then goes on to pump in additives, preservatives, colouring and synthetic vitamins that are stressors to already stressed systems. As consumers we have a very important role to play in the food we all buy and eat. We need to demand quality; learn to understand labels; refuse to buy foods that are over-processed. Change will only happen if we consumers collectively insist upon it.

Ever sceptical, many of my personal friends – some of them in the medical profession – continue to doubt the obvious problems that intensive agriculture and the food industry are creating. Some go even further in denying the true extent of the role that good nutrition plays in good health. In many other cultures, mostly oriental, people eat well due to centuries-old observation, benefiting from curative and preventative 'food medicine'. In Britain, most orthodox doctors still consider nutritional medicine a 'complementary' aid to good health, whereas it is actually *essential*. Many doctors – and patients – equate health with 'not being ill', and being ill is construed in largely clinical terms. Often marginal but persistent health imbalances cannot be immediately identified, and again are dismissed as 'not being ill'. In this way we limit our capacity for life, for its enjoyment, quality and longevity.

THE RECIPES

All the ideas and recipes here represent a healthy balance and harmony. They are also easy to recreate at home. They are obviously inspired by my eastern French background, but also contain many southern French and Mediterranean influences, as well as Asian concepts. The latter two are not passing fashions, but are here to stay, as both encapsulate most of the criteria of good nutrition. The oils used are healthy, there is a preponderance of vegetables, and small but flavourful portions of protein-rich meats and fish. I've even included *foie gras*, that luxurious food associated in many minds with over-indulgence and wealth. Expensive it may indeed be to purchase, but in no way does it conflict with the healthy principles in the generality of recipes here. For I have observed, and it has been scientifically proved, that the diet of South-West France, dominated as it is by duck and goose fat, does not have deleterious effects on health, rather the opposite, and many people of that region live long and healthy lives. *Foie gras*, in fact, is now championed as a Superfood (see Appendices). As an organ meat, liver is rich in all the B vitamins, many nutrients which are needed for metabolism in general, and also fat, hence its good properties.

All the ingredients used in this book are available in any supermarket. You will also notice that I use wholemeal pasta and unrefined rice and other grains because they retain their complete nutritional and therapeutic properties; you can obviously substitute these with refined products, but they will be far less nutritious. On the advice of Dr Monro, I have also replaced sugar with fructose (see page 266), an easy substitution which offers greater benefits.

This book does not pretend to be an infallible bible satisfying the complex demands of every individual. But few of the recipes require more than twenty minutes' preparation and will suit most people and most lifestyles, whether you are a child, a party animal, a driven executive, or a dedicated gourmand. (In fact, we have indicated the types of food suitable for and nutritional needs of each of what we have called 'seven nutritional "ages" of man'.) Each of the sections in the book not only aims at improving your nutrition, but also suggests how joyful, stimulating and relaxing really 'good' food can be.

Brillat-Savarin also wrote that, 'The pleasures of the table belong to all times and all ages, to every country and every day: they go hand in hand with all other pleasures, outlast them and remain to console us for their loss.' That warm eternal resonance is something everyone can achieve on a daily basis with this book – rediscover the simple creative act of cooking and the joy of eating, both of them linked with good nutrition.

I wish you *bonne santé*, and many friends around your table.

TEN BLANC COMMANDMENTS FOR WHOLESOME AND GOOD FOOD

1   Use only the freshest food, organic where possible, to ensure wholesomeness and nutritional quality.

2   Eat a varied diet and go on enjoying meat so long as you eat lots of vegetables and fruits. And two or so glasses of red wine a day is not frowned upon.

3   Try to use as little sugar and salt as possible in cooking, particularly in your children's meals. Let them grow up with more refined palates than us – and free from our health problems.

4   Remember that a simple omelette and a glass of red wine is, in all ways, a superior alternative to a Mars bar and a can of cola.

5   At least three times a week, invite your child(ren) to your table so that you dine together, facing each other instead of the television.

6   Get into the habit of reading food labels when shopping in order to avoid the nastiest additives and excess salt and sugar.

7   Date your prepared dishes when you are freezing or refrigerating them. Most food poisoning happens at home.

8   When dining out, take your children with you sometimes. They will enjoy it.

9   You are a consumer. All food revolutions have been achieved through the collective action of consumers. Be critical and demanding. You have a role to play, so be responsible.

10   Cooking is an act of love, so give the best to your family.

HEALTH ON YOUR PLATE

JEAN MONRO

Man's history as a cultivator of his food is relatively recent, dating from 8,000 years ago – about half a per cent of man's existence as man. In biological terms, this is not a long time. In these same terms, man's technological revolution is very young, only a couple of centuries old. Man now manufactures his foods, preserving, refining and adulterating them with artificial contaminants and additives. But in a period of only two hundred years, he can hardly be expected adequately to adapt to his own revolution.

Man has developed over the years to be omnivorous – and this evolution should be respected. He was thought to be herbivorous two million years ago, largely eating fruit and nuts. After that, he became a hunter and ate meat. Our forefathers' trials of food sources, like those of rudimentary science, were of simple trial and error: sometimes they selected a food, found it tasted good and consumed it; sometimes they selected a food and perished, for not everything that is natural is tolerated by the human body. Although our planet is so rich in natural foods, our vegetable and fruit intake is often limited to a very few plant families, many of which have some edible members and others which are poisonous. Even now very few people would risk eating plants which have been avoided for centuries.

There are numerous families within plant species whose poisonous and friendly members flourish equally. For example, among the fungi, yeast is an extremely important food and source of vitamins. Most mushrooms are a good source not only of flavour but of vitamins and iron, but some fungi produce mycotoxins which are among the most toxic, naturally occurring substances we know. (The death-cap mushroom can cause death by poisoning very swiftly.) Even the most commonly eaten fruits can contain poisonous components, such as the pips of apples and pears, or the kernels of apricots. This is not meant to be alarmist, merely to underline the benefits of respecting centuries-old observations which have proved life-saving.

Animals, unless very slow, rely on their abilities of fight or flight for protection rather than developing poisonous tissue to avoid predation, as some plants do. Therefore, animal flesh can be eaten with impunity, unless it is contaminated, such as with the heavy metal, mercury, which accumulates in fish swimming in polluted water. As we are at the end of the food chain, if food animals cannot rid themselves of a pollutant, then we can ingest it too. However, animals act as a filter of any toxic material they might consume in their food and therefore can also act as a filter for us – and are thus certainly safer than some toxic plants. Animals which harbour infection such as tuberculosis, however, can pass the infection on (hence the need for tuberculin-tested cattle).

There is accumulating evidence that, over time, some of the chemicals we now use in growing and processing our foods are toxic. Fertilisers, herbicides and growth enhancers can build up and cause stress in the human body, causing many illnesses and allergies. Organic produce, as well as being free from contaminants, tastes so much better than crops which have been sprayed with chemicals. The selection of plants, farming sites, agricultural techniques, whether using organic methods or agrichemicals, farm maintenance and harvesting all play a part in making healthy – or unhealthy – food. The transportation, storage, processing and packaging of food will affect its quality too. The food industry's use of additives is important, as are the availability to the body of nutrients, and the effects of cooking, heat, cold, light and air in storage. Similar considerations apply in the raising of animals for food.

And we overprocess foods too. Nature provides with a food the very qualities, vitamins and minerals which are needed for its own metabolism, and it is these that are removed by modern refining. White flour contains no fibre, which is removed to be processed into a separate commodity, bran; ironically this is added back to the diet to correct modern bowel complaints such as constipation, irritable bowel syndrome and diverticulitis – *complaints probably caused by its absence*. The wheat germ too has been removed, and with it much of the plant's concentrated nutrients such as proteins, Vitamin E, chromium, magnesium and manganese. These are all needed in the metabolism of carbohydrate which is largely what remains in white flour.

Preparation and storage of foods is extremely important as well, because there needs to be an understanding of the chemical changes which can occur and which may be toxic. Over-charred foods can be carcinogenic. Foods from the Chenopodiaceae family, including beetroot, can cause poisoning if they are cooked and cooled in the water in which they were cooked, or if cooked for too short a time. Kidney beans can be poisonous if they are not boiled, the water discarded, and the beans subsequently boiled again. And potatoes which have sprouted or are green should not be eaten; they contain solanine, a poison produced by the nightshade family, to which the potato belongs. There is a thin line between what is innocuous and what is toxic, even among apparently 'edible foods'.

A basic rule of good diet is never to concentrate on any particular food. If we eat a varied diet, then no natural – or unnatural – toxin can accumulate, and all our enzyme systems are used in balance. The best diet is a varied one, and the best food natural and unadulterated. Nature is the only infallible expert.

The recipes chosen and developed for this book are based on several sound principles. Firstly, all ingredients have been carefully selected for their nutritional value, and to complement each other. Secondly, they reflect the huge variety which provides the balance necessary for the healthiest diet. We have not cut out meat because of its fat content, or butter – we have simply used all ingredients in moderation.

When I first met Raymond I was delighted to find how many of the very best ideas of nutrition were already incorporated in his menus at Le Manoir aux Quat' Saisons. Genuinely 'good' food must be the true mark of a great chef. The richness and exquisite flavours of his dishes comes from fresh, organic vegetables and meat.

THE BASIC COMPONENTS OF DIET

The most basic components of diet are called macronutrients and micronutrients. Macronutrients are proteins, carbohydrates (and fibre) and fats. Micronutrients are vitamins and minerals.

PROTEIN

Protein is more plentiful in our bodies than any other substance but water. Protein comprises half the dry body weight, including most of the muscle mass, skin, hair, eyes and nails. It is the main structure and ingredient of our cells, and the enzymes that keep them running. Immunity to disease relies on protein; in fact, the immune system and its antibodies are largely composed of protein.

The building blocks of protein are amino acids. Twenty of these are vital for the body, and some of these are known as *essential* because they cannot be synthesised by the human body, and must be supplied by the diet. Without these essential amino acids constantly entering the body, the rate of new protein formation would slow down and, in extremes, stop altogether.

Proteins are the basis of all life. Those from meat, fish, eggs and cheese are known as complete proteins, containing the correct proportion of amino acids. Vegetable proteins are not so complete but by *combining* foods such as grains and pulses or nuts, more complete protein can be created.

CARBOHYDRATE

Carbohydrate foods are energy foods, and include sugars and starches (and indeed dietary fibre as well, see below). They are formed from simple sugars, among which are glucose (found in most foods), fructose (primarily found in fruit) and galactose (dairy produce). Sucrose is refined from cane and beet sugar, and in digestion breaks down to glucose and fructose.

These simple sugars form interlinking chains, to make complex carbohydrates – the starches, such as grains, cereals and pulses and the foods made from them (bread, pasta, etc.) – plus vegetables and fruits. Complex carbohydrates have to be broken into simple sugars for absorption, the most significant of which is glucose. We require only limited stores of carbohydrate, for any not immediately used by the body is stored as glycogen in the liver and muscles, and anything in excess is converted into fat.

The structure of simple sugars in the food, the soluble fibre and fat content of a food determines the rate at which carbohydrate is metabolised and glucose enters the bloodstream. The more rapidly this occurs the more 'glycaemic' the food, with a propensity to raise blood sugar. This is undesirable because as blood glucose levels rise, the pancreas secretes insulin to enable the liver and muscle cells to store the glucose. As insulin levels increase, so blood sugar levels fall. Once they fall below a critical level, the brain, which needs glucose to function, becomes impaired. This is hypoglycaemia, an affliction which can cause many unpleasant symptoms, in children particularly.

Of all the simple sugars, only glucose can be released directly into the bloodstream, which is why glucose-rich carbohydrates, such as sugar, and sugary cakes and biscuits, are highly glycaemic. Fructose and galactose must first be converted to glucose and therefore enter the bloodstream at a slower rate. This is a very slow process with fructose especially, which is why fructose-containing carbohydrates, primarily fruits, are low glycaemic foods.

Glycaemic foods are primarily foods that have been refined, and include sugar (honey, sucrose, maltose, glucose, sweets, chocolates), white flour (bread, pasta, biscuits, refined cereals, often with added sugar), and refined rice (white).

Unrefined carbohydrates, those which are not glycaemic, include wholewheat products (brown bread, brown flours, wholewheat pasta), maize and other whole grains, wild rice, unpolished brown rice, fruit, vegetables, legumes and pulses such as lentils, beans and peas. These should play a significant part in any healthy diet.

FIBRE

Fibre consists mostly of cellulose, a substance forming plant cell structures (skins, husks, peels etc.). It is non-digestible carbohydrate, and is not absorbed by the body. But fibre has another use: it slows the rate of absorption of other carbohydrates into the bloodstream. The higher the fibre content of a carbohydrate, the less glycaemic it is. Fibre-rich foods include whole cereals (bran in particular), pulses, dried fruit, baked potatoes (with skins) and green leafy vegetables. Peel fruit and vegetables as thinly as possible, or not at all.

The second biggest killer cancer is bowel cancer. This could be prevented by a good intake of fibre on a daily basis (vegetables, fruits and cereals). Insoluble fibre increases bulk in the stool, and encourages more fluid retention in the stool and healthy action of the bowel in general. Soluble fibre slows and moderates absorption of sugars and glycaemic foods.

FAT

Fats come from animals, fish and vegetable sources. Animal fats are largely what is called saturated. We need some of these – including cholesterol (although our bodies actually manufacture this, see page 14) – to make our own hormones like cortisone and the sex hormones, but too much can be provided in the diet which is quickly converted to body fat (as are excess glycaemic foods).

Vegetable fats, which include olive oil, nut and seed oils, are unsaturated fats. These contain the essential fatty acids which the body cannot manufacture, and which are necessary for making healthy tissues (and may indeed reverse the effects of saturated fats). The best are mono-unsaturated fats such as olive oil. Some fish oils are also unsaturated and essential, and can be protective.

There are two main families of unsaturated fatty acids: the Omega-6 and Omega-3 series. The chart following shows where they are to be found.

FATTY ACID	FOOD SOURCE	ENRICHED SOURCE
Omega-6 – linoleic acid (LA)	Vegetables, seeds and nuts and oils	Corn, pumpkin, sunflower, sesame, corn, walnut, soya and wheatgerm oils
Omega-6 – gamma linolenic acid (GLA)	Seeds, nuts and oils	As above, also evening primrose oil, borage oil, blackcurrant oil
Omega-3 – alpha linolenic acid (ALA)	Seeds and nuts	Flax seed, linseed, pumpkin, and evening primrose oil
Omega-3 – eicosapentaenoic acid (EPA)	Seafood	Fish oils
Omega-3 – docosahexaenoic acid (DHA)	Seafood	Fish oils

When fats are eaten with carbohydrate, they slow the rate of absorption of the carbohydrate into the bloodstream. The biggest deficiency of all in the West is of essential fatty acids. So fat *is* necessary for good health, but an excess intake, however, is not recommended.

MICRONUTRIENTS: VITAMINS AND MINERALS

Macronutrients – proteins, carbohydrates and fats – require micronutrients, which include vitamins and minerals, to work efficiently. All the vitamins are essential for good general health, and at least fifteen minerals are considered to be necessary. Most of these are obtained from the diet. Micronutrients also clear 'rust' from the body, oxidised material which is irritating to the tissues and contributes to disease – the notorious 'free radicals'. Antioxidants – especially Vitamins A, C and E and glutathione with the mineral selenium – help to rid the body of these.

Then there are other components of foods which are neither standard vitamins nor minerals, which I will call vita-nutrients in Superfoods – chemicals with vital protective, life-giving or energy-giving properties like proanthocyanidins in red wine and the essential oils in herbs (see the Appendices). Of particular importance are the carotenoids and bioflavonoids. The carotenoids – which include beta-carotene, the principal precursor of Vitamin A – are pigments found in foods of plant origin, particularly in orange and dark green vegetables and fruit. They are protective in many ways, primarily in their antioxidant action. Bioflavonoids are naturally occurring compounds – among them citrin from citrus fruits and rutin from cereals – which prevent the destruction of Vitamin C by oxidation, which strengthen capillary walls, inhibit blood clotting and are helpful in hypertension and allergy control.

THE CHOLESTEROL DEBATE

Cholesterol is a substance naturally manufactured by the body, and it is found in most animal tissue. Cholesterol is transported in the body attached to chemicals called lipoproteins, which can be high density (HDL) or low density (LDL). LDL deposits cholesterol in the membranes of the arteries while HDL mobilises cholesterol. It is when LDL cholesterol is oxidised that atherosclerosis occurs. Olive oil protects LDL from oxidation and the body from heart disease and strokes. Wine also increases the activity of HDL. Sugars, however, can lead to an increased oxidation of LDL.

Raymond has already alluded to the diet of the French in southern France. They have a diet high in fat, eating *foie gras* (fatty goose liver) among other cholesterol-rich foods, and yet they suffer less illness. They also smoke heavily, and drink. Despite these indulgences they have one-third the incidence of coronary heart disease suffered by Americans and Australians. This dispels the cholesterol myth. The explanation seems simple: it is not cholesterol in the diet which causes coronary heart disease, but sugar. For, despite their seemingly damaging lifestyle, they take in their diets one-sixth the amount of sugar eaten elsewhere in the West, eating a fresh, natural and organic diet, not processed foods from the packets, tins and jars we tend to have in the UK and elsewhere. They shop daily for fresh vegetables, and consume garlic and onion which contain potent bioflavonoids (see above). The red wine they consume contains other chemicals which benefit vasculature, and their diet includes large amounts of mono-unsaturated olive oil. The French also use many herbs in their cooking: rosemary, for instance, is one of the most powerful antioxidant herbs in the vegetable kingdom. They rarely drink milk but have fermented and cultured dairy products such as cheese and yogurt (in the latter, the lactose sugars have been fermented out and the bacteria are good for health). The French often *overeat*, but there is a low incidence of obesity. Stress is low, and mealtimes are enjoyed with the family.

There is clear evidence that populations living in the Mediterranean countries have a longer life expectancy than northern Europeans. Genetic or racial factors do not explain these differences in society, because migration studies have proved no correlation. The major causes of death in the affluent societies – cardiovascular disease, cancer and digestive disorders – have very different incidence rates in different European countries, and the differences depend on diet. The most likely explanation is that a more relaxed lifestyle and a high fruit and vegetable consumption protect against disease.

Elsewhere in the world the cholesterol debate rages equally. In northern India the people consume a large amount of *ghee* which is clarified butter, a high cholesterol fat, yet they have one-fifteenth the incidence of heart attacks of southern Indians. Those in the south are often total vegetarians eating no animal fats, but they eat coconut oil, a saturated fat, and margarine instead, as well as large amounts of sweetmeats. The fats in margarine are hydrogenated polyunsaturated fatty acids (PUFA), which oxidise quickly, and are known to increase LDL. Butter, despite its fattening reputation, is actually much healthier than margarine.

THE IMPORTANCE OF BALANCE

What I am trying to explain, through this brief account of nutritional principles, is the importance of understanding a little about the body's own balancing acts. In my life's work, I have observed the imperative role played by correct nutrition in restoring the body to health. The integration of protein, carbohydrate and fat in a meal results in a correct balance of blood sugar. Some 25 per cent of the population has an elevated insulin response to carbohydrate, and they very easily gain fat; 25 per cent have a blunted response and can eat a large quantity of carbohydrate without gaining fat; and between these two is the 50 per cent which has a fluctuating response, which depends on the diet. What we require are small meals with the correct ratio of protein, carbohydrate and fat.

To provide ourselves with these macronutrients, we need small quantities of fish, cheese, eggs, milk and meat, the high protein foods. We also need carbohydrates, and all vegetables and fruits contain micronutrients, minerals, vitamins, and many other valuable components. Calorie intake can have varied effects depending on body type and the rate at which an individual breaks down food.

The following chart contains a summary of dietary recommendations for health in general.

GOOD	GOOD IN MODERATION	BAD
Fresh seasonal fruits, vegetables, salads and nuts	Some lean meats	Sugar and sugar-containing foods
Cold-pressed mono-unsaturated oils e.g. olive oil	Eggs and lean poultry	Margarine and PUFA
High soluble fibre foods: oats, rice, barley, fruits	Wholegrain breads and cereals	Salt in excess
Garlic and onions	Sun-dried fruits (see Superfoods)	Processed food and food additives
Fresh fish and seafood	Natural bio yogurt and butter	Unfiltered coffee
	Red wine	Stress

Balanced meals and snacks should be based on whole foods taken from each of the four main food groups: grains; milk, milk products and fats; proteins; fresh vegetables and fruits.

GROUP I   GRAINS

2 daily servings

E.g. wholemeal biscuits, bread or crispbreads; brown rice; muesli; oat porridge; wholewheat pasta.

GROUP II   MILK, MILK PRODUCTS AND FATS

2–4 daily servings

E.g. milk, butter, cheese (soft and hard), cream, vegetable oils (olive and walnut especially, but also corn, groundnut, safflower and sunflower), yogurt.

GROUP III   PROTEINS

At least 2 daily servings

E.g. beans (dried) with grains, beef, chicken, eggs, oily fish (herring, mackerel, sardine, tuna, salmon), offal (kidney, liver), meat (beef, lamb, pork, poultry), nuts, game (rabbit, venison etc.), seeds (good sprouted as well), shellfish and white fish (cod, monkfish etc.).

GROUP IV   FRESH VEGETABLES AND FRUIT

4–5 or more daily servings

Some vegetables and fruit should be eaten raw. Hard vegetables may be cooked. It is wise to eat some raw food at every meal because this supplies an important enzyme which is destroyed by cooking. Also more vitamins and minerals are retained in the food if uncooked; some water-soluble vitamins are actually lost when the food is cooked.

A meal made up entirely of foods taken from each of these four groups should furnish a good supply of minerals, essential fatty acids and vitamins as well as proteins and carbohydrates, provided that a minimum loss of nutrients occurs in storage, preparing, cooking and serving.

THE PRINCIPLES OF A HEALTHY DIET

To assist in the provision of the best health I have listed the principles of a basic diet, some of which of course cross over with the 'Ten Blanc Commandments' on page 9.

1 Eat fresh unrefined food, organic if possible.

2 Enjoy a varied diet.

3 Take pure fruit juices, unsweetened.

4 Drink bottled or filtered water.

5 Avoid artificial flavourings, colourings and additives.

6 Avoid processed foods.

7 Try not to consume too much preserved, tinned, smoked, heavily salted or pickled foods.

8 Avoid instant drinks such as fizzy cordials; they contain sugar, preservatives and artificial sweeteners.

9 Minimise sugar and sugary foods, e.g. sweets, cakes, biscuits and tinned fruit in syrup.

10 Take small, regular meals rich in protein, vegetables and fruits.

11 Cook in a healthy way – boiling, roasting, poaching, steaming and pan-frying in a minimum of fat.

12 Try to include Superfoods containing 'vita-nutrients' in your diet.

Throughout all the recipes in this book Raymond will highlight these principles. The most important ingredient of perfect health is happiness, however, and we should all enjoy our food. With my French friend, I wish you *bon appétit* and the very best of health.

SEVEN NUTRITIONAL 'AGES' OF MAN

It is undeniable that at certain times of life our bodies have differing nutritional needs. With the invaluable help of Dr Monro, I have examined a number of 'ages' or categories, and detailed lifestyles and foods that might be suitable.

TOUJOURS LES VACANCES

Our twenties and thirties are addictive, exciting years when ambition, deadlines, enthusiasms and a quest for success seem all-consuming. We have always lived with these sorts of stresses, but it is only when stress becomes relentless that it threatens the body, making us feel like cornered animals with no opportunity to escape. The adrenal glands start speeding metabolism, and this automatically alters the rate at which our body uses its resources. Replenishment of these is imperative in those leading a high-powered lifestyle, and this involves resting, away from the stress.

A balance between sleep and a busy life is also crucial. Good sleep at night is vital in many ways, but good sleep also releases melatonin, the main hormone that automates our hormone system. It is created in the body during darkness, and dwindles during the time we are exposed to light. Melatonin is the most powerful of antioxidants (see page 14), 500 times more powerful than Vitamin C.

Good nutrition is particularly important at this time. A diet high in Superfoods will encourage the removal of toxins from the body and protect from stress-related illness. However, stress can actually be *induced* by one food – by *sugar*. The quick 'fix' of a sugary chocolate bar at your desk is not a good idea; a good snack and some fruit will satisfy your appetite, your taste buds and your digestion, and will keep you going for much longer.

How and when you eat is as important as *what* you eat. Take ten minutes to sit down. Enjoy a glass of wine. Let your mind focus on something (or someone) you like. Now savour every bite. After all, these are the best years of your life.

BREAKFASTS
All recipes

SNACKS
All sandwiches, dips and spreads
Mascarpone, spinach and mushroom pitta pizza

SOUPS
Clam and vegetable soup
Curried cream of cauliflower soup with coriander purée
Tomato and roast pepper soup

SALADS AND STARTERS
Salad of mixed sprouts with olive oil and lemon
Crab and avocado salad with coconut and mint
Grilled tuna with aubergine and tomato *confit*
Quail with warm chilli vinaigrette
Soused mackerel with beetroot salad

FISH AND SHELLFISH MAIN COURSES
John Dory with artichokes, carrots and fennel
Baked mackerel with artichoke and tomato *salsa*
Pan-fried oysters with mushroom purée and chervil
Pan-fried sea bream with marinated vegetables
Pasta with mussels, courgette and chilli
Red mullet with *tahini* sauce and crab couscous
Braised squid with rice pilaff
Steamed salmon and *pak-choi* with Tabasco oil

MEAT, POULTRY AND GAME MAIN COURSES
Breasts of mallard with butternut squash
Calf's liver with red onion marmalade
Chicken with flageolet beans
Daube of beef with orange
Duck with broccoli and cauliflower
Poussin with a vegetable broth
Roasted quail with polenta and wild mushrooms

DESSERTS
Baked tamarillos with hazelnut *crème anglaise*
Chocolate *pot à la crème*
Pineapple and blueberries with chickpea pancakes

MÉNAGE À TROIS

As a man, I may be occasionally insensitive to female needs, but never as a chef. As both, I have often wondered why pregnant women have cravings for extraordinary things like petrol fumes, gherkins and chalk. It would be wonderful if I could, in this book, develop those odd cravings into longings for the very best of foods!

Preconceptual care is now a whole nutritional speciality for hopeful *mamans*, but men also have a nutritional role to play when trying to conceive. Our old friend Casanova was quite right about the aphrodisiac oyster – zinc-rich foods are said to be excellent for sperm production. In Denmark, organic farmers consuming their own produce had twice the sperm count of men eating commercially grown products. So practising an organic lifestyle could be a real act of love towards your imminent new family.

Good food is vital, both preconceptually and during pregnancy. Once pregnant, a new *maman* should eat five portions of well-washed fruit and vegetables a day. She should eat plenty of calcium-rich foods such as milk, yogurt and cheese; soft-boned fish such as tinned salmon and sardines are also a good source of calcium. Oily fish like sardines are high in essential fatty acids, protecting against heart disease (and may help to prevent stretch marks). *Maman* will benefit from lots of Superfoods and minerals (see Appendices). Iron, folic acid (which prevents birth defects such as spina bifida) and iodine are essential (fish and kelp are excellent sources of the latter). Avoid soft cheeses because of the risk of listeriosis; raw eggs could be a problem too because of the risk of salmonella. Do not drink alcohol during pregnancy: babies could be born underweight. And never smoke.

Prospective mothers should demand to be spoiled. If his cooking is so awful that he can't manage the simple recipes in this book, get him to bring you to Le Manoir instead!

BREAKFASTS
All recipes

SNACKS
All sandwiches, dips and spreads

SOUPS
Chicken and soy broth
Soup of sugar-snap peas with broad beans and lovage

SALADS AND STARTERS
Beetroot and watercress salad
Bulgar wheat and cucumber salad
Octopus with green beans, onions and feta
Oysters with soured cream and red wine vinaigrette
Pan-fried *foie gras* with wild mushrooms and rocket

FISH AND SHELLFISH MAIN COURSES
Cod with clams and Jerusalem artichokes
'Gigot' of monkfish with tomato and pepper sauce
Grilled sea bass with fennel and lemon
Squid, Parmesan and parsley salad

MEAT, POULTRY AND GAME MAIN COURSES
Roasted best end of lamb
Breast of free-range chicken in a vegetable *nage*
Grilled quail with chickpeas and fennel
Guinea fowl with butter beans and radicchio
Loin of venison with butternut purée and red wine pear chutney
Poussin with herbs and braised aubergine
Spring *navarin* of lamb with *fricassée* of beans
Stuffed beefsteak tomatoes Maman Blanc

DESSERTS
Caramelised apples in spiced wine
Chocolate and raspberry *torte*
Mandarins and gooseberries in their own juices

LA BONNE FEMME

Without pretending to understand everything about women, I know that they have special nutritional needs. Hormones are crucially related to nutrition, and women's lives are dominated by hormonal activity – the years of the monthly cycle, through child-bearing, and into menopause. Vitamin B6, essential fats and Superfoods (see Appendices) can help stabilise the menstrual cycle and relieve the symptoms of pre-menstrual tension (PMT). The recent debates on hormone replacement therapy (HRT) have highlighted soya as an excellent source of naturally occurring oestrogen; the contribution this makes to regulating hormonal activity can alleviate hot flushes and other menopausal symptoms.

A woman has irregular calls on resources throughout her life – the demands of a baby during pregnancy, for instance – and these can all be perfectly well accommodated provided she eats correctly and well. If she has not done so, however, she may develop some deficiency diseases, the commonest of which is osteoporosis. To protect against this, she should ensure she always has good sources of calcium and Vitamin D (see Appendices).

Women are men's future, their saviours, mothers, sisters and wives. In all the battles between the sexes, they generally win, being more powerful . . . However, there is one proven route to pleasing females while restoring male pride: to cook for them. Being more particular and sensitive to details, they know how to appreciate – and their discrimination makes one's triumph all the greater. Satisfaction all round.

BREAKFASTS
All recipes

SNACKS
All sandwiches, dips and spreads
Artichoke, rocket, sardine and Parmesan pitta pizza

SOUPS
Chicken and soy broth
Clam and vegetable soup
Soup of sugar-snap peas with broad beans and lovage

SALADS AND STARTERS
Chicken liver salad with lentils and orange
Pan-fried *foie gras* with watercress and hazelnut salad
Smoked salmon with creamed rocket, cucumber and chilli
Tiger prawns with fresh mango and rocket

FISH AND SHELLFISH MAIN COURSES
Pan-fried salmon with courgettes and radish vinaigrette
Sardines with olive tomato vinaigrette and chickpea purée
Turbot steaks with chanterelles and spinach

MEAT, POULTRY AND GAME MAIN COURSES
Calf's liver with red onion marmalade
Cutlet of pork with a mushroom soy *jus* and *pak-choi*
Roasted guinea fowl with *confit* of beetroot
Loin of lamb with couscous and red pepper chutney
Spring *navarin* of lamb with *fricassée* of beans
Pork cutlets with lentils
Tofu lasagne

DESSERTS
Oeufs à la neige
Roasted bananas with lychees and passionfruit
Strawberries and raspberries with cream

LES ENFANTS TERRIBLES

As a parent, you are blessed with the greatest creative challenge and joy of all: the unadulterated palate. Through cooking for your child, your own sensual expression, you are helping to form a new sense of taste, probably for life. However, nuances of flavour also come from our sense of smell; the largest part of the brain is related to smell, and it is our longest-term memory. By letting him or her smell good food cooking, and tasting it, your child will retain those early memories for ever.

Babies have to learn to enjoy tastes. This is wonderful for you and baby, and you can experiment and create! From about five months, purée 'whole' fruits, vegetables and selected grains, organic where possible. Try gravies of beef or other meat, but restrain your urge to regale them with buttery, wine-infused sauces. Food must not be too rich, and flavours should not be too strong. So use little salt or sugar: a baby's kidneys cannot metabolise the former, and the latter is completely empty in a nutritional sense. And cook in healthy ways – steaming, poaching etc., rather than frying. Until at least nine months, most babies cannot tolerate too much fat, egg white, whole nuts or hot spices. From nine to twelve months you can introduce cheese, beans, yogurt, *fromage frais*, wholewheat bread and pastas, casseroled meat and well-cooked egg white. Cow's milk could be drunk after one year, and never offer skimmed or low-fat dairy products; children need the fat as well as the calcium.

By the age of five, most children have fixed ideas of what they like and dislike. They also need a lot of food (they could be a restaurateur's dream), three times as much, per unit of weight, as adults, which makes for three meals and two to three snacks a day. Exploit this opportunity to introduce an enormous variety of healthy snacks. Encourage them, as I do all my friends (of whatever age), to use their hands. Let them communicate with food with all their senses, which is real enjoyment and understanding of food. Let them dip bread into cold-pressed olive oil, which has a similar calorific count to, but less cholesterol than, butter.

My peasant childhood was gloriously free of today's relentlessly chemical environment and culture. Animal studies have shown that certain food colourings frighteningly accelerate the release of certain brain chemicals; other studies demonstrate that some children react dramatically to food colourings. Science also now recognises that hyperactive children are suffering from exposure to lead from car exhausts and pollution, leading to learning and behavioural problems. Inner-city children are obviously most at risk.

These risks are exacerbated by poor nutrition and by a lack of vitamins and minerals. As I have always feared (I refuse to enter any form of hamburger bar), diets high in junk food are a poor source of Vitamins B1 and B6, as well as zinc and magnesium.

In my experience, all children love nutritious food. It is very refreshing to share in their enthusiasm, and I find them a wonderful audience. Children appreciate beauty as much as, if not sometimes more than, jaded adults. Always garnish their meals, if only with the most basic fresh herb sprig. Most of all, I think it is sinful to make healthy food boring for children.

BREAKFASTS

All recipes

SNACKS

All sandwiches, dips and spreads
Mozzarella, courgette and tapenade pitta pizza
Mozzarella and tomato pitta pizza

SOUPS

Butternut squash and lemon soup
Leek and chervil soup
Tomato and roast pepper soup

SALADS AND STARTERS

Chicken and snowpea salad
Egg mayonnaise
Pan-fried *foie gras* with pears and honey
Ricotta and spinach croquettes
Wholemeal pasta with ham and Gruyère cheese

FISH AND SHELLFISH MAIN COURSES

Grilled tuna with borlotti beans and salsify
Salmon fishcakes with tomato sauce
Steamed cod with watercress purée
Crab cakes with courgette chutney

MEAT, POULTRY AND GAME MAIN COURSES

Stuffed beefsteak tomatoes Maman Blanc
Chicken breast with coconut and cardamom
Glazed lamb shanks
Veal escalope with spinach, peas and mustard cream

DESSERTS

Baked pears with almonds and honey
Chocolate mousse
Figs and strawberries with balsamic vinegar
Poached cherries with maple syrup and roasted almond ice-cream
Roasted peaches with peach and lavender *coulis*
Strawberries and raspberries with cream

LE BON VIVEUR

Let's eat, drink and be merry.

Even up to twenty years ago, most British *bons viveurs* were beset with health problems. And today Great Britain still tops the chart for cardiovascular problems, heart attacks etc., the results of too much heavy, cream-laden food, sugar and not enough vegetables, good fibre and fruit. Things are changing though, and expense-account restaurants, the traditional haunt of the *bon viveur*, are now offering better food lifestyles, under the influence of the French (of course), the Italians and Asians. However, steak and kidney pudding, a British classic, is actually an excellent food, rich in protein and folic acid, but few would benefit from eating it at every meal. Moderation and balance are the key to health. With a little knowledge of nutrition, one can live and enjoy most of the pleasures of life, especially good food and good wine. For instance, a simple idea, but one that is a basic nutritional precept, is to start a meal with a salad of raw vegetables: this stimulates the digestion beneficially and, of course, reduces the need for over-indulgence thereafter!

As a spry, wiry Frenchman (sorry, false modesty really is a quintessential English quality!), I was brought up in a family of *bons viveurs* who are all slim, fit and happy. This is in keeping with the national gastronomic tradition. The typical French *bon viveur*, consuming a diet of fresh food and *foie gras*, washed down with the best wine, often lives to a ripe and healthy old age. France enjoys the lowest average individual body weight of all western countries, and the least incidence of cardiovascular disease. And all this whilst digesting up to two three-course meals per day, following a breakfast of *chocolat* and *croissants*.

If this all seems irritatingly unfair or contradictory, you can blame the most ubiquitous of 'nutritional' deceptions: the great calorie lie, that 'obesity results from a diet too high in calories'. We all know obese people whose problems persist despite severe 'dieting' or starvation. There may well be temporary weight loss, but the body will guard itself against perpetual rationing by simply reducing its daily needs to less than the new reduced calorie intake. The surplus calories will still be stored daily, as body fat, resulting eventually in weight gain. You cannot out-manoeuvre Nature. Luckily for us, the body *does* reach a natural point of satiation, but only once it receives enough *nutrients*, not calories. It is time to stop this obsession with calories, and to return to what sustains food traditions: common sense.

The British are changing. I see them in my restaurants, tie-less, hat-less and smiling and truly enjoying their food. Nowadays they even kiss their hellos, and embrace surprised Frenchmen! There is a wonderful new mood of sensuality. A British *bon viveur* is no longer characterised by his or her indiscriminate drinking and eating, but by an enthusiastic appreciation of beautiful food and wine.

Science today reassures us that no connoisseur of the good life need deny themselves: with a little knowledge of nutrition, one can eat, drink, be merry *and* healthy.

BREAKFASTS
All recipes

SNACKS
All sandwiches, dips and spreads

SOUPS
Crab chowder
Curried cream of cauliflower soup with coriander purée
Curried mussel and vegetable soup

SALADS AND STARTERS
Chicken liver with raw beetroot and port vinaigrette
Grilled tuna and aromatic vegetables with oregano oil
Haricot bean, cherry tomato and basil salad
Salad of celeriac, poached egg, *lardons* and *frisée*

FISH AND SHELLFISH MAIN COURSES
Braised sea bream and mussels with saffron potatoes
Brill in tomato juice with capers and parsley
Mackerel with mashed potatoes and hazelnut vinaigrette
Monkfish glazed with honey and soy sauce
Red mullet with green olive *tapenade* and courgettes
Roasted scallop, rocket and Parmesan salad
Tiger prawns, smoked aubergine purée and radicchio

MEAT, POULTRY AND GAME MAIN COURSES
Asian *pot-au-feu*
Roasted best end of lamb
Duck breasts with broccoli and cauliflower
Rabbit with spring vegetables
Breast of free-range chicken in a vegetable *nage*
Lambs' kidneys with lettuce and peas
Wood pigeon with pan-fried radicchio
Soy-marinated chicken breasts with cucumber vinaigrette
Pan-fried ribeye steaks with mustard pepper crust

DESSERTS
Gratin of figs with mascarpone
Grilled figs with raspberries and port
Pink grapefruit in Campari with mascarpone sorbet
Rhubarb with blood oranges, opal basil and mascarpone

LES VÉGÉTARIENS

By nature, we are omnivorous, not vegetarian. Our system is designed to metabolise meat, fish, vegetables, grains and many other foods. Yet I understand why many people become vegetarian.

Traditionally, chefs have Olympian ignorance about – and a great prejudice against – vegetarians, but I find it quite pleasing that one eats as one thinks and as one lives. Most of my vegetarian guests and friends are actually extremely appreciative of their food, and very knowledgeable. They have to be, as they need to follow essential nutritional guidelines in order to have a completely balanced diet.

Vegetarians can be deficient in nutrients, particularly protein. Lacking the complete proteins of meat, they have to combine the incomplete proteins of grains, beans and lentils to make complete proteins or eat some of these with some protein from dairy produce or eggs. Some possible combinations are: legumes (lentils, peas or beans) with nuts; legumes with all grains; fresh vegetables with rice or other whole grains; fresh vegetables with mushrooms.

There are other risks as well. In Britain, strict Hindus and others who eat no animal food can be vulnerable to osteomalacia and rickets, caused by a deficiency of Vitamin D. Vitamin B12 only occurs in animal products, and a deficiency can result in pernicious anaemia in vegans (vegetarians who do not eat milk, eggs or cheese).

Vegetarian food can be sumptuous, healthy and simple to cook. We have had a vegetarian *à la carte* menu at Le Manoir for many years. Partly, it is a spur to my kitchen: meat dishes offer big tastes, but vegetarian dishes are as varied, and can be as intense, requiring a lighter hand and a finer palate. There are many vegetarian dishes in this book that you will enjoy (and not just in the vegetarian chapter).

BREAKFAST

All recipes except for those with fish or meat

SNACKS

All sandwiches (except for one pitta bread one), dips and spreads
Mozzarella, courgette and tapenade pitta pizza
Mozzarella and tomato pitta pizza

SALADS AND STARTERS

Asparagus, celery and leek salad
Beetroot and watercress salad
Bulgar wheat and cucumber salad
Cep and *mâche* salad with Parmesan
Classic potato salad
Egg mayonnaise
Haricot bean, cherry tomato and basil salad
Jerusalem artichoke and chervil salad
Ricotta and spinach croquettes

MAIN COURSES

All the main courses in the vegetarian chapter

DESSERTS

Lemon verbena creams with lemon syrup
Coffee and caramel *pot à la crème*
Poached peaches with lemongrass syrup

NE REGRETTE RIEN

The most extraordinary 'fan' letter I ever received began with an erotic description. In sensual detail, I was offered the image of an upper lip lifting in pleasure, while small teeth sliced into a plump white peach. The juices spilled over, and lightly smeared the chin of my seductress, a 70-year-old lady.

And why not? The latter part of our lives should be a time to bloom, not fade. A common error is to assume that we need less food after middle age and less *good* food. I know too many older people who are unused to caring only for themselves: they eat meagre meals and often resort to convenience food. In fact, at this time we require better-quality protein, and a diet rich in fish and meat will supply many amino acids necessary to boost health. Calorie intake, however, should be tailored to exactly what is needed to stay fit. Antioxidant foods – those which contain Vitamins A, C and E, plus selenium and zinc – will have some anti-ageing effect. To maximise a healthy lifespan, a moderate amount of aerobic exercise should be taken, and stress should be avoided at all costs.

People evolve. By the second half of our lives, we should have honed the art of joy to a fine point. That means a refined understanding of our bodies, minds and affections. And what better testament to this than a fine meal shared with friends and family?

BREAKFASTS

All recipes

SNACKS

All sandwiches, dips and spreads

SOUPS

Chilled turnip and rocket soup
Almond and garlic soup

SALADS AND STARTERS

Carpaccio of sea bream with flavours of the Orient
Marinated sardines with chickpeas
Salad of mushrooms and anchovies
Sautéed squid with chickpeas and *pak-choi*

FISH AND SHELLFISH MAIN COURSES

Mackerel with a potato and rocket salad
Roast halibut with asparagus, spring onions and sage oil
Scallops with chickpea cakes and yellow pepper vinaigrette

MEAT, POULTRY AND GAME MAIN COURSES

Braised rabbit legs with potatoes and peppers
Chicken with flageolet beans
Confit of duck with spinach and tomato *confit*
Lambs' kidneys with lettuce and peas
Pan-fried ribeye steaks with mustard pepper crust
Cutlet of pork with a mushroom soy *jus* and *pak-choi*
Poussin with herbs and braised aubergine
Poussin with a vegetable broth
Roasted quail with polenta and wild mushrooms
Wood pigeon with pan-fried radicchio

DESSERTS

Confit of plums in red wine with vanilla
Melon soup with red wine *granita*

BASIC
RECIPES

THE FOLLOWING INCLUDE A NUMBER OF BASIC

RECIPES WHICH ARE USED THROUGHOUT THE

BOOK — STOCKS, PURÉES, SAUCES, ETC.

WHITE CHICKEN STOCK

This is a subtle and flavourful stock which is useful in many ways, in soups and in sauces.

MAKES 1 LITRE

Planning ahead

The stock can be stored in the fridge for 3 or 4 days, or for up to 2 months in the freezer.

2kg raw free-range chicken wings or raw chicken carcasses, chopped
15g unsalted butter
1 small onion, peeled and finely chopped
white of 1 small leek, finely chopped
1 small celery stalk, finely chopped
100g button mushrooms, finely sliced
1 garlic clove, peeled and crushed
10 white peppercorns, crushed
200ml dry white wine (optional)
1 litre cold water
1 bouquet garni

Method

Sweat the chicken wings in the butter for 5 minutes without colouring. Add the chopped vegetables, garlic and crushed peppercorns, and sweat for a further 5 minutes. Pour in the wine (if using), and boil to reduce by one-third.

Cover with the cold water, bring back to the boil and skim. Throw in the *bouquet garni* and simmer for 1 hour, skimming from time to time. Strain through a fine sieve and leave to cool, before chilling or freezing.

RB's note

The carcasses of roasted chickens may be used instead of raw.

BROWN CHICKEN STOCK

Because the chicken has been browned first, the flavours of the stock, and its colour, are deepened and intensified.

MAKES 450ML

Planning ahead
The stock can be made in advance and refrigerated for 1 week, or frozen for 3 weeks.

1.5kg raw free-range chicken wings or raw chicken carcasses, finely
   chopped
100ml groundnut oil
1 medium onion, peeled and finely chopped
1 garlic clove, peeled and crushed
100g mushrooms, chopped
6 black peppercorns, crushed
½ bay leaf
1 sprig of fresh thyme
approx. 900ml water

Method
Preheat the oven to 230°C/450°F/Gas 8.

In a large roasting pan, heat the oil until smoking, then over the highest heat, brown the chicken wings or carcasses for 8–10 minutes, stirring occasionally with a wooden spoon. Add the chopped onion, garlic and mushrooms and cook for another 5 minutes until lightly coloured. Cook in the preheated oven for 20 minutes until the chicken wings and vegetables turn a rich brown. Spoon out the excess fat and discard. Add the peppercorns, bay leaf and thyme and stir.

Deglaze the pan with 200ml of the water, scraping up all the caramelised bits from the bottom of the pan. Transfer this liquid, the bones and vegetables to a saucepan, cover with the remaining water, and bring to the boil. Skim, then simmer for 20–30 minutes. Strain off the juices and skim off any fat. Cool before chilling or freezing.

VEGETABLE NAGE

A clear scented stock made from vegetables, herbs and spices.

MAKES 500ML

Planning ahead
The stock can be kept in a covered container in the fridge for 2–3 days, or for several weeks in the freezer.

½ onion, peeled and finely chopped
white of 1 small leek, finely chopped
1 carrot, peeled and finely chopped
¼ celery stalk, finely chopped
peelings of 1 fennel bulb, finely chopped, or some fennel seeds
2 garlic cloves, peeled and finely chopped
4 pink peppercorns
1 star anise
8 white peppercorns, crushed
zests of 1 lemon and 1 orange
1 sprig of fresh thyme
500ml cold water
a small bunch of fresh chervil or coriander, chopped
6–8 coriander seeds
100ml dry white wine

Method
Put all the vegetables, spices, zests and thyme into a large saucepan and pour in the cold water. Bring to the boil and skim, then simmer for about 10 minutes.

Add the chopped herb and coriander seeds, pour in the wine, and simmer for a further 2–3 minutes. The gentle acidity of the wine will 'lift' the stock.

Take the pan off the heat and leave uncovered for 5–6 hours so that the flavours infuse. Strain the stock through a fine conical sieve, pressing with a ladle, into a storage container. Seal and chill or freeze.

BASIL PURÉE

This needs no introduction. Add Parmesan or Pecorino cheese if you prefer, pine kernels or walnuts if you want, a little lemon or lime juice if you like. It will always be wonderful.

2 bunches of fresh basil, leaves picked
50ml extra virgin olive oil
2 garlic cloves, peeled
salt and freshly ground black pepper

Method

Mix all the ingredients together in a mortar and pestle or in a food processor, and blend as finely or as coarsely as you like. Season to taste. Conserve covered with olive oil, or freeze.

TOMATO CONFIT

These semi-dried tomatoes are very useful in a number of ways – particularly delicious with the halibut on page 187.

SERVES 4

4 large, ripe but firm plum tomatoes (approx. 120g each)
3 tbsp olive oil
3 sprigs of fresh thyme, leaves picked
rock salt and freshly ground black pepper

Method

Preheat the oven to 120°C/250°F/Gas ½.

Blanch the tomatoes in boiling water for about 30 seconds, then refresh in iced water. Remove immediately they are cold, and core them and peel off the skins. Cut the tomatoes in half lengthways. Remove the seeds.

Place the tomato halves on an oven tray and sprinkle with the olive oil, thyme, salt and pepper. Dry in the low oven for 3–4 hours, then remove from the oven. Cool.

If not using straightaway, store in the oil they were cooked in.

ROCKET PURÉE

The beauty of this rocket purée (and all its family), is that you can keep it in the fridge for a couple of weeks. So, if you like, make two or three times the amounts specified in the recipe.

1 bunch of fresh rocket, shredded
100ml olive oil
juice of 1 unsprayed lemon
50g pine kernels
salt and freshly ground black pepper

Method
Simply blend the rocket with the oil, lemon juice and pine kernels, then season to taste.

TOMATO SAUCE

Make the sauce smooth by sieving it, or leave it chunky – a texture which is preferable in some dishes.

SERVES 4

Planning ahead
The sauce may be made well ahead of time.

400g tomatoes, cored and roughly chopped
50ml olive oil
1 small onion, peeled and finely chopped
2 garlic cloves, peeled and finely chopped
50ml extra virgin olive oil

Method
Heat the olive oil in a saucepan, add the chopped onion, and sweat for 3–4 minutes until transparent. Add the chopped tomatoes, cover and simmer for 4–5 minutes. Add the crushed garlic and boil, uncovered, for 2–3 minutes, stirring from time to time. Liquidise the sauce, then push through a fine sieve. Cool and then whisk in the extra virgin olive oil.

CHICKPEA PANCAKES

A good pancake, especially with one of the breakfast toppings, made with an unusual flour – from chickpeas.

MAKES ABOUT 6–8 X 10–12CM PANCAKES

Planning ahead
The pançakes may be prepared in advance and reheated.

1 egg
175ml milk
2 tsp honey
olive oil
80g fine chickpea flour
a pinch of salt

Method
Beat the egg together with the milk, honey and 3 tbsp of the olive oil. Sieve the chickpea flour into another bowl with the salt, and gradually mix in the egg mixture until it is totally smooth. Strain through a fine sieve. Leave to rest for 30 minutes at room temperature.

To make the pancakes you can either do individual ones in a small non-stick skillet or pan, or smaller versions by pouring small spoonfuls of the mixture into a larger pan, four or five at a time.

Brush the pan with some olive oil and heat. Pour in a small ladleful of the batter and rotate the pan to make a thin pancake. Fry for 30–40 seconds, then turn over with a spatula and fry the other side for the same length of time. Make six to eight larger pancakes in this way.

Especially good with *Dried Figs in Honey* (see page 51).

Variations
The pancakes may be made savoury by omitting the honey. They could then be served with bacon, eggs or grilled oily fish.

BULGAR WHEAT PASTRY

This pastry is an interesting alternative to wholemeal pastry, and is useful in vegetarian main courses.

Planning ahead

The pastry may be made a day in advance if wrapped and refrigerated. Allow to come to room temperature before rolling.

400g bulgar wheat
400ml water
4 tbsp olive oil
½ tbsp salt
a little wholemeal flour

Method

Place the bulgar wheat into a bowl. Boil the water, pour it over the bulgar, cover with a piece of clingfilm, and leave to stand for an hour until the bulgar absorbs the water.

Blend together the bulgar, oil and salt in a food processor until it forms a ball, adding a little wholemeal flour if the dough is too sticky, then wrap and chill until needed.

When rolling, do so on a surface dusted with a little wholemeal flour.

COOKED DRIED PULSES

Pulses are easy to cook, they just take a little care and lots of time. If you like, you could replace freshly cooked pulses with tinned pulses; they require no cooking, just rinsing, draining and heating through if necessary.

The following recipe is suitable for chickpeas, haricot and flageolet beans, borlotti and kidney beans, and butter beans. All must be boiled first, preferably for about 10 minutes, to get rid of potential toxins.

SERVES 4

250g dried pulse of choice (to achieve about 400g cooked)
salt and freshly ground black pepper

Method

Soak the pulses for between 4 and 12 hours, preferably overnight (24 hours for butter beans). It is difficult to be completely accurate about this, as it depends on the age of the pulse. Always buy from an outlet with a rapid turnover to ensure they are as 'fresh' as possible.

Drain the pulse, rinse, and cover with plenty of fresh water. Bring this to the boil, and boil for a few minutes, preferably 10 in the case of kidney beans, then drain. Rinse the pulse, cover again with fresh water and bring back to the boil. Turn the heat down, cover the saucepan, and cook at just below simmering point for 1–1½ or 2 hours for the beans, 2–3 hours for butter beans, up to 4 hours for the chickpeas. Drain when cooked and soft.

Only add seasoning when the pulse is cooked, as salt can harden the skins.

RB's note

It is as impossible to be completely accurate about cooking time as it is about soaking time: it all depends largely on the age of the pulse and the manner in which it has been stored. The best way, as with everything in the kitchen, is to constantly taste and check as you go along.

BREAKFASTS

Breakfast is vital, as it is the first meal of the day and the most important. So often these days it is ignored, replaced by some strong coffee and stress. Your state of mind for the rest of the day is affected by the way in which you begin it, so start a little earlier, organise your thoughts, sit with your family, and consume the mixture of proteins, fats, carbohydrates and vitamins that is essential.

This chapter has recipes for special cooked weekend breakfasts, various nutritious drinks and toppings for mueslis, bio yogurts and pancakes. It also gives suggestions for making your own muesli, one that will give you a good combination of tastes and nutrients.

RB

It has often been shown that people who do not have breakfast perform less ably when asked to do tasks which require hand/eye coordination and speed of reflex action. And we all know the hollow, hungry feeling that hits mid-morning after no breakfast or an inadequate one. This interferes with concentration and thus effectiveness. It is particularly important for schoolchildren to eat a good breakfast that will sustain them happily through until lunchtime.

The best foods for breakfast are carbohydrates – grains which are unrefined and whole, and fruits. Because the latter contain fructose, they are more slowly metabolised so that there is no quick glycaemic burst, induced by the release of simpler sugars into the body. The fruits are generally provided whole so that they have their own fibre; this also slows the absorption of carbohydrate and helps in good digestion. A nut accompaniment, or milk or yogurt, will add a protein component to the meal, and these, like good fats, will also help to slow absorption of sugar. We are creatures of routine; too often we have the same breakfast every day. It is important to vary your breakfast.

JM

HOME-MADE MUESLI

The important thing to remember here is that you need to create a balance between the proteins, carbohydrates and fats.

PROTEIN AND FAT

These come primarily from nuts and seeds, among them hazelnuts, peanuts, almonds, walnuts, pecans, sunflower seeds, sesame seeds and linseeds. If you like, you could roast them slightly to intensify their flavour or, if you do not like having whole nuts to contend with, you could chop or grind them. It is essential that you keep the papery skins on the nuts.

Proteins can also come from the dairy or soya liquids you might use on your muesli (see Liquids, below).

CARBOHYDRATE

These are the grains primarily, among them rolled oats, wheat flakes, barley flakes, millet flakes, buckwheat flakes, puffed wheat and puffed rice. Choose those which are unrefined and have no additives or added sugar.

Dried fruits provide another form of carbohydrate energy, as well as extra flavour and nutrients. It is worth looking for the quality varieties as they can transform a simple muesli into a sublime one. Health-food stores now stock a good variety (choose those which have not been sugared or sulphured), or you could make your own. Wash and cut the fruits in half, then place them on cooling racks over the tops of trays; bake in the oven at about 60°C (the very lowest it will go), either overnight or to the point that you prefer, a little dryer or softer than the bought variety.

You can choose from dried apricots, prunes, bananas, sultanas, raisins, currants, figs, pears, apples, pineapple and mango. You can now find dried cherries, blueberries and cranberries as well.

LIQUIDS

You can use cows', goats' or ewes' milks, or bio or live yogurts made from them. Soya milk and yogurt are good too. You could make your own nut milks by liquidising about 100g shelled nuts with 500ml milk of choice or water, and then straining through a fine sieve. Coconut milk, preferably unsweetened, can be bought.

Juices can moisten your muesli – or simply accompany it! There are now some very good and fairly cheap juicers on the market which give you room to experiment. Try juices made from celery and apple; carrot, orange and ginger; tomato; Granny Smith apples; pears; apricots; peaches; and pineapple.

When fruits or vegetables are juiced, of course, they lose quite a proportion of their fibre content (left behind in the machine). They still provide good nutrients, though.

FRUIT AND NUT TOPPINGS

Here are a few simple toppings that you could use on bio yogurt and muesli, or on pancakes (see page 40). They are not intended to be served on their own as they would not supply sufficient protein. All make enough for about two servings. If you have some left, just cover, put in the fridge and use the next day.

PRUNES WITH BLOOD ORANGES AND CARDAMOM

400g fat prunes, stoned
juice and grated zest of 2 unsprayed blood oranges
3 tsp maple syrup
2 cardamom pods, crushed

Method

Boil the blood orange juice and zest with the syrup and cardamom. Add the prunes and bring back to the boil. Simmer for 2 minutes, then either serve straightaway, or allow to cool.

DRIED APRICOTS WITH LEMON AND HONEY

400g dried apricots
grated zest and juice of 1 unsprayed lemon
2 tsp liquid honey

Method

Boil the lemon juice and zest with the honey. Add the apricots and bring back to the boil. Simmer for 2 minutes then either serve straightaway, or allow to cool.

PEARS WITH VANILLA

2 medium Comice or William pears, cored and cut into large dice
3 tbsp fructose
3 tbsp water
$\frac{1}{2}$ vanilla pod, halved lengthways and scraped

Method

Heat a frying pan and sprinkle over the fructose. Add the pears and the water, and sauté over a high heat for 3 minutes. Transfer to a bowl and add the scraped vanilla seeds.

SULTANAS IN APPLE JUICE AND GINGER

300g sultanas
250ml apple juice
1 x 3cm piece of fresh root ginger, peeled and grated

Method

Bring the apple juice to the boil with the ginger, add the sultanas and bring back to the boil.

BANANAS WITH COCONUT MILK AND PALM SUGAR

2 large bananas, peeled and diced
100ml unsweetened coconut milk
20g palm sugar
grated zest and juice of 1 unsprayed lime

Method

Boil the coconut milk with the palm sugar, add the bananas and bring back to the boil. Add the lime juice and zest.

NUTS WITH HONEY

This is a great way to get kids to eat nuts that aren't salted and pre-packed. Any unpeeled nuts will do.

100g nuts
groundnut oil
3 tsp liquid honey

Method

Brush a non-stick tray thoroughly with a little groundnut oil. Heat a frying pan, spoon in the honey and add the nuts. Sauté for 2–3 minutes until they begin to caramelise lightly. Transfer them to the non-stick tray and spread them out. Leave to cool.

PAPAYA OR MANGO WITH MINT

1 very ripe papaya or mango
4 fresh mint leaves (optional), finely sliced

Method

Peel and stone the papaya or mango. Dice one half and purée the other, then mix both together with the mint.

DRIED FIGS IN HONEY

150g dried figs, halved
4 tsp liquid honey
2 tbsp extra virgin olive oil
2 tbsp water
juice of $\frac{1}{2}$ unsprayed lemon

Method

Melt the honey with the olive oil, water and lemon juice, add the figs and cover. Cook over a gentle heat for 5 minutes until the figs have plumped up. Serve hot.

RASPBERRY CRÈME FRAÎCHE

This can be made either with *crème fraîche*, mascarpone cheese or *fromage frais*, and the raspberries can be substituted by strawberries or blackberries.

150g raspberries
100g *crème fraîche*
2 tbsp fructose

Method

Crush the raspberries lightly with a fork then mix with the *crème fraîche* and fructose.

MARINATED STRAWBERRIES

This is a good way of getting the best out of strawberries, and again they may be substituted by any berries you have available. To enhance it even more, you could make a small amount of strawberry purée and add that too. If you are lucky enough to be able to procure wild strawberries, I am already jealous!

150g strawberries
lemon juice to taste
fructose to taste

Method

Cut the strawberries into even-sized pieces and place them into a bowl. Mix with the lemon juice and fructose, cover and allow to marinate for about 30 minutes at room temperature.

MEDLEY OF FRUIT WITH FROMAGE BLANC

SERVES 4

200g strawberries, quartered
juice of 1 unsprayed orange
40g fructose
300g *fromage blanc* (40% fat)
4 sprigs of fresh mint

Method

Mix the orange juice and 30g of the fructose with the strawberries. Reserve. Spoon the fromage blanc in the middle of plates or bowls of muesli, or on a pancake, and arrange the fruit around. Decorate with sprigs of mint and sprinkle with the remaining fructose.

Variations

Of course the *fromage blanc* can be replaced by *crème fraîche* or Greek yogurt. The possibilities with the fruits are endless.

SMOOTHIES AND SHAKES

These are a healthy, quick and fun way to start the day. All make approximately enough for one large glass. Simply prepare all ingredients as appropriate, then place in the blender and liquidise until smooth.

PAPAYA AND PASSIONFRUIT

$^1/_2$ ripe papaya, peeled and seeded
pulp of 2 passionfruits
100ml grapefruit juice
1 tbsp fructose

BANANA AND YOGURT

2 bananas, peeled
200ml bio yogurt
2 tsp liquid honey

PINEAPPLE AND COCONUT

$^1/_4$ small, very ripe pineapple, peeled
250ml unsweetened coconut milk
$^1/_2$ vanilla pod, halved lengthways and scraped

APRICOT AND APPLE

150g dried apricots, soaked until plump in 200ml apple juice
150ml milk

KIWI FRUIT AND YOGURT

It is very important to use extremely ripe kiwi fruit for this otherwise it will be too acidic. Equally it must be drunk immediately, or it will oxidise.

3 ripe kiwi fruit, peeled
100ml bio yogurt
100ml milk
2 tbsp fructose

COOKED BREAKFASTS

The following recipes mostly involve animal protein, and are a little more substantial. They also involve slightly more work, so could be something to treat yourself to at the weekend.

POTATO PANCAKES WITH SMOKED SALMON

This is a bit of a weekend special. If you feel up to it on Friday night, you could make the pancakes, keep them in a cool place, and heat them up on the Saturday morning in plenty of time for breakfast in bed.

SERVES 2

1 large starchy potato, weighing about 400g
1 small bunch of fresh chives, finely snipped
salt and freshly ground black pepper
2 tbsp groundnut oil
100ml soured cream
6 fine slices of cold-smoked salmon
1 unsprayed lemon (optional)

Method
Preheat the oven to 180°C/350°F/Gas 4.

Peel the potato, wash and then grate it. Fold the grated potato into a tea towel and squeeze out as much of the water as possible. Transfer to a bowl and mix with half of the snipped chives then season with salt and pepper. Heat a small non-stick frying pan with 1 tbsp of the groundnut oil, place half the grated potato/chive mixture into it, press down well with a spatula and fry over a medium to high heat for 2 minutes. Turn with the spatula and fry for a further 2 minutes on the other side. Transfer to a tray then repeat the process with the second half of the mixture. Place the pancakes in the oven for 5 minutes.

Mix the soured cream with the second half of the chives and season with salt and pepper.

Remove the pancakes from the oven, spread with the soured cream, top with the salmon, and garnish with a lemon half if you like.

RB's note
Remember to choose a variety of potato with the necessary starch to hold the pancake together.

POACHED EGGS WITH ASPARAGUS AND SPINACH

SERVES 2

4 very fresh free-range eggs, poached (see page 58)
10 asparagus spears, trimmed
salt and freshly ground black pepper
30g butter
150g spinach, leaves picked and washed
1 sprig of rosemary, leaves picked and very finely chopped

Method

Blanch the asparagus in plenty of salted water for 4–5 minutes, until *al dente*. Keep warm.

Heat the butter in a large pan and sauté the spinach for a minute until wilted. Divide this between two plates, add the asparagus and top with the eggs. Sprinkle the rosemary over the top and serve with a good grind of black pepper.

POACHED EGGS WITH MUSHROOMS ON TOAST

Here I'm going to try and give you directions for the perfect poached egg. It is a technique made easy by the use of vinegar which firms up the egg white slightly and helps to keep its form.

SERVES 4

8 free-range eggs
6 tbsp white wine vinegar
750ml water
rock salt and coarsely ground black pepper
4 tbsp olive oil
600g mixed wild mushrooms, washed and cut if necessary
4 thick slices of *pain de campagne*

Method

Mix 4 tbsp of the vinegar with the water. Break the eggs carefully into this and leave them to sit for about half an hour.

Bring a shallow pan of water to boiling point with the remaining vinegar and salt to taste. Turn the heat down as low as possible. Pour as much cold water as possible away from the eggs (without losing them down the sink), then pour the eggs into the hot water. Poach them, turning occasionally and never allowing the water to come near boiling point, for 5–7 minutes, depending on how soft you like them cooked.

While the eggs are cooking, heat a frying pan with the olive oil and sauté the mushrooms for 3–4 minutes. Season well with salt and black pepper.

Toast the *pain de campagne*. Spoon the mushrooms on top of this, top with the poached eggs and sprinkle with salt and black pepper.

OMELETTE AUX FINES HERBES

There are many fillings, stuffings and toppings for omelettes, but I believe that in this case the simplest is the best. The fragrant combination of chervil, tarragon and chives is quite delightful. There has been a lot written on the making of a perfect omelette but for me it is simple: fresh free-range eggs, a non-stick pan and never allowing the omelette to wait.

Nutritional note

Eggs are a complete food. As they contain protein, fat, carbohydrate and all the nutrients necessary for a new life, they are therefore one of the best foods available. However, they do not have significant Vitamin C. Provided there is another source of this in the diet for the day, then an egg dish is an excellent starting point. Adding herbs and green vegetables provides fibre, flavour and micronutrients such as magnesium.

SERVES I

3 large free-range eggs
salt and freshly ground black pepper
1 tbsp snipped fresh chives
1 small fresh tarragon leaf, snipped
10 sprigs of fresh chervil, snipped
20g unsalted butter

Method

Beat the eggs together with a little salt and pepper then add the snipped herbs. Heat a small non-stick pan with the butter until it begins to foam. Pour in the egg and herb mixture and wait about 10 seconds until it begins to set around the outside of the pan. Pull the set part inwards and allow the liquid to go towards the outside; continue this for about 2 minutes until the omelette has formed completely but is still slightly liquid in the centre. Fold the sides towards the centre and turn out on to a plate. Serve immediately.

OEUFS SUR LE PLAT

There are special dishes in which to make this that are flat with little ears but, failing this, you can use ramekins. A few wholemeal toast soldiers are recommended.

SERVES 2

2 large free-range eggs
1 large tomato, cored and sliced
salt and freshly ground black pepper
6 tbsp double cream
4 fresh tarragon leaves, sliced

Method

Preheat the oven to 180°C/350°F/Gas 4.

Spread the tomato slices around the bases of the dishes. Season them well with salt and black pepper then break an egg over the top of each. Spoon over the cream and sprinkle over the tarragon. Place in the preheated oven for 8–10 minutes until the egg has just firmed up, and serve immediately.

OEUFS SUR LE PLAT WITH OLIVE OIL

2 large free-range eggs
1 large tomato, sliced
2 tbsp extra virgin olive oil
4 fresh basil leaves, finely shredded

Method

Preheat the oven to 180°C/350°F/Gas 4.

Arrange the tomato slices as described above, then break the eggs over them. Top with the olive oil and shredded basil, then bake for 8–10 minutes until the egg has just firmed up. Serve immediately.

SCRAMBLED EGGS WITH SPINACH AND BASIL PURÉE

Good scrambled eggs must be cooked very slowly to ensure their creamy texture.

SERVES 2

4 large free-range eggs
50ml milk
2 tbsp olive oil
200g young spinach, tough stalks removed
salt and freshly ground black pepper
4 tbsp *Basil Purée* (see page 38)
a few fresh basil leaves to garnish

Method

Mix the eggs together with the milk then pour into a small, non-stick saucepan. Cook, stirring constantly for about 5 minutes, over a low heat until the mixture begins to thicken.

Meanwhile, heat a large frying pan with the olive oil and sauté the spinach for about 2 minutes, just until it wilts, then season well. Mix the basil purée in with the eggs, when they are nearly cooked to a creamy consistency. Season to taste, and serve on top of the spinach. Garnish with the basil leaves.

GRILLED KIPPERS WITH PARSLEY BUTTER

SERVES 2

2 plump kippers
50g butter, softened
1 small bunch of fresh parsley, leaves picked and finely chopped
grated zest and juice of 1 unsprayed lemon
$^1/_2$ unsprayed lemon, cut into wedges

Method

Heat the grill to its highest setting.

Mix the butter with the parsley and lemon zest and juice. Spread this over the kippers and place them into a shallow pan. Put about 2 tbsp of water into the bottom of the pan, and place it under the grill for about 6–8 minutes. Serve with wedges of lemon, if you like.

KIPPERS ON CHICKPEA PANCAKES

SERVES 2

$^1/_2$ recipe *Chickpea Pancakes* (see page 40)
2 kipper fillets, cut into 3cm pieces
4 free-range egg yolks
2 tbsp double cream
1 large shallot, peeled and finely diced
1 small bunch of fresh parsley, leaves picked and finely chopped

Method

Preheat the oven to 180°C/350°F/Gas 4.

Make 2 large pancakes as per the recipe. (You will have more batter than you need.) Lay them on individual ovenproof plates or on a baking tray.

Scatter the pieces of kipper around the outsides of the pancakes. Place the egg yolks in the centre with the double cream, and sprinkle the shallot and parsley over the top. Bake in the preheated oven for 6–7 minutes until the egg yolks are just set. Devour.

Following page:

Grilled kippers with

parsley butter

Variations

Fresh mackerel or sardine fillets could replace the kipper.

BEEFSTEAK TOMATO PIPÉRADE

A version of a great classic.

SERVES 2

2 large beefsteak tomatoes, cored
2 small shallots, peeled and thinly sliced
1 garlic clove, peeled and thinly sliced
1 red pepper, seeded and cut into strips
2 tbsp olive oil
salt and freshly ground black pepper
2 tbsp *Basil Purée* (see page 38)
4 large egg yolks
2 tbsp grated Parmesan

Method

Preheat the oven to 180°C/350°F/Gas 4.

In a covered pan, sweat the sliced shallot, garlic and pepper in the olive oil for 10 minutes.

While these are cooking, slice the tops off the tomatoes and just enough off the bottoms that they sit flat. Scoop out most of the flesh and seeds from the insides of the tomatoes, chop then add to the red pepper mixture. Season this well, then transfer it to an ovenproof dish with a few spoonfuls of water.

Top this with the tomatoes. Put a spoonful of basil purée into each tomato, followed by an egg yolk and finally some of the Parmesan. Bake in the oven for 10 minutes (or until the yolks are set, if you prefer), then eat immediately.

PAN-FRIED MUSHROOMS IN ROLLS

SERVES 2

200g mixed mushrooms
20g butter
juice of $\frac{1}{2}$ unsprayed lemon
2 large wholemeal bread rolls, lids cut off and centres scooped out
50ml double cream
salt and freshly ground black pepper
10 fresh flat-leaf parsley leaves, sliced

Method

Preheat the oven to 180°C/350°F/Gas 4.

Melt the butter in a frying pan. Add the mushrooms and sauté for 2 minutes. Add the lemon juice and a couple of tablespoons of water, cover the pan and cook for a further minute.

While this is cooking, heat the bread rolls and their lids in the oven. Add the cream to the mushrooms and reduce slightly. Season to taste then spoon the mushrooms and their sauce into the bread rolls. Sprinkle with parsley and top with the lids.

BAKED BANANAS WITH VANILLA

SERVES 2

2 large very ripe bananas
2 tsp liquid honey
juice of 1 unsprayed lemon
a few drops of vanilla essence
bio yogurt or ricotta cheese

Method

Preheat the oven to 180°C/350°F/Gas 4.

Cut two pieces of foil about 30cm square. Peel the bananas then place them on top of the foil. Spoon over the honey, squeeze over the lemon and sprinkle with vanilla essence. Close up the sides of the foil and seal well. Place on a tray in the preheated oven for 5 minutes, then eat piping hot with a little yogurt or ricotta.

SNACKS

'Snacks' are equated with fast food in most people's minds, but you don't have to enter a burger joint to enjoy a quick fix of something delicious. There are now many specialist shops that can make your life much easier. You can get instant and good fresh food just by stopping by your local delicatessen. Vegetables such as artichokes, mushrooms and sun-dried tomatoes in olive oil can be bought bottled. If you serve them with herbs, and eat either at room temperature or slightly warmed through with a little salad of sprouts or leaves, they make a wonderful light supper on their own.

The selection of wholemeal breads available now is quite astonishing. Those with herbs, spices or nuts can transform simple sandwiches into something very special. Pitta bread can be stuffed with a fresh filling or halved to make pizzas. You can make a variety of sauces or salsas and dips which are great with bread, or with *crudités* – raw pieces of vegetable such as carrot, celery, pepper etc. So, a relaxing excursion to a deli, baker and grocer can become a treat at lunchtime or after work.

RB

Mention 'snacks' to many people, and they think of a bag of chips or crisps, and things that you can pop straight from freezer to toaster or oven. But snacks are important, occasionally, in extremis, replacing a proper meal. They're especially relevant to children, who need more 'topping up' than adults, and we should always ensure that what they eat, at any time, is healthy and nutritious.

For instance, served along with bread, many foods in this chapter, such as the chickpea purée, will form a good source of protein. The bread used, whether in sandwich or as pizza base, is a good source of carbohydrate, complementing the accompanying vegetable and protein ingredients. If a dip or salsa is accompanied by raw crudités *and breads, a snack food becomes even more valuable. Using olive oil instead of butter in many of the dishes such as the pizzas, is more Mediterranean in feel, and could encourage children to enjoy these healthier tastes. Almost all the dishes here contain Superfoods (see Appendix).*

JM

PITTA PIZZAS

Using these recipes you can see how easy it is to experiment and make your own preferred toppings. These are quick and delicious pizza alternatives that leave just enough time for a shower while they cook. All of them serve two people.

For the bases, wholemeal pitta bread is available now in almost any supermarket; for the tomato sauce you can either use our recipe for chunky *Tomato Sauce* (see page 39), or one of the many quality bottled sauces that can now be found, especially at specialist Italian stores.

MOZZARELLA AND TOMATO

This is only for the summer when your tomatoes are at their best.

1 large wholemeal pitta bread, cut in 2 across the centre
4 tbsp chunky *Tomato Sauce* (see page 39)
1 mozzarella cheese, approx. 120g
4 large ripe plum tomatoes, cored
1 small bunch of fresh basil (keep a pot on the windowsill)
4 tbsp olive oil
freshly ground black pepper

Method
Preheat the oven to 200°C/400°F/Gas 6.

Spread the tomato sauce over the top of the pitta. Slice the mozzarella and tomato to the same thickness. Layer them on top of the pitta bases. Tear the basil and sprinkle over, then douse with the olive oil and bake for 15 minutes. Give a good grind of black pepper, and serve.

Previous page, clockwise from top left:

Chilli aubergines; Tomato salsa (centre); Avocado dip; Braised red peppers; Tapenade; Bottled artichokes; Chickpea purée; Marinated shiitakes

ARTICHOKE, ROCKET, SARDINE AND PARMESAN

This can be made with or without the tomato sauce.

1 large wholemeal pitta bread, as page 71
6 bottled artichokes, drained and cut in half
6 fresh sardine fillets
1 large bunch of rocket, leaves picked and coarsely chopped
sea salt and coarsely ground black pepper
100g Parmesan, sliced in shavings with a vegetable peeler
4 tbsp olive oil

Method

Preheat the oven to 200°C/400°F/Gas 6.

Alternate the artichokes and the sardine fillets across the pitta base, then top with the chopped rocket. Sprinkle with sea salt and coarse black pepper. Cover with the Parmesan shavings and douse with the olive oil. Bake for 15 minutes.

MASCARPONE, SPINACH AND MUSHROOM

1 wholemeal pitta bread, as page 71
2 tbsp olive oil
2 garlic cloves, peeled and crushed
100g spinach, leaves picked, washed and shredded
100g button mushrooms, washed and sliced
100g mascarpone cheese
1 small bunch of fresh parsley, leaves picked and chopped
salt and freshly ground black pepper
4 tbsp chunky *Tomato Sauce* (see page 39)

From top to bottom:
Mascarpone, spinach and mushroom; Mozzarella and tomato; Artichoke, rocket, sardine and Parmesan

Method

Preheat the oven to 200°C/400°F/Gas 6.

Warm the olive oil, and add the garlic, spinach and mushrooms. Sauté over a high heat for 2 minutes without colouring, then decant into a colander and allow to cool. Once cooled, stir in the mascarpone and chopped parsley and season well.

Spread the tomato sauce across the pitta bread, then top with the spinach mixture, bake for 15 minutes, and serve.

CARAMELISED ONION, ANCHOVY AND OLIVE

1 large wholemeal pitta, as page 71
2 very large onions, peeled and finely sliced
2 garlic cloves, peeled and crushed
4 tbsp groundnut oil
salt and freshly ground black pepper
$^1\!/_2$ quantity *Anchoïade* (see page 76)

THE GARNISH
6 black olives, cut in half and stoned
4 anchovy fillets, cut in half lengthways

Method
Preheat the oven to 200°C/400°F/Gas 6.

Sweat the onion and garlic in the oil for 15 minutes without colour until totally soft. Raise the heat then, stirring constantly, caramelise the onion and garlic for 5 minutes, giving them a golden brown colour. Season and set aside.

Spread the *anchoïade* across the halved pitta bread, then top with the caramelised onion. Decorate with the halved olives and anchovies. Bake for 15 minutes, and serve.

MOZZARELLA, COURGETTE AND TAPENADE

1 large wholemeal pitta, as page 71
2 medium courgettes
160g mozzarella cheese
1 small bunch of fresh oregano, leaves picked and chopped
6 tbsp extra virgin olive oil
salt and freshly ground black pepper
$^1/_2$ recipe *Tapenade* (see page 76)

Method

Preheat the oven to 200°C/400°F/Gas 6.

Slice the courgettes and mozzarella about 1cm thick. Mix them with the oregano, olive oil and a little salt and freshly ground black pepper.

Spread the *tapenade* across the pitta bread, then top with the courgettes and mozzarella, alternating the slices. Bake in the preheated oven for 15 minutes, and serve.

SPREADS AND OTHER TASTES

These are not really recipes for any set moment or for any set number; they are more to take bits of perhaps as part of a lunch buffet, perhaps as pasta sauces or spread on wholemeal toast, *bruschetta* or *crostini*. They are all handy, healthy snacks that keep well in the fridge for days.

TAPENADE

Tapenade is traditionally made with capers and anchovies, but can be made with just the olives, garlic and olive oil.

100g stoned black olives
2 garlic cloves, peeled
50ml extra virgin olive oil

Method
Purée together in a food processor. You will not need to season it.

OLIVES IN ORANGE JUICE

200g calamata olives
200ml orange juice, reduced by half
1 small bunch of fresh oregano, leaves picked and finely chopped
50ml extra virgin olive oil

Method
Mix all the ingredients together.

ANCHOÏADE

50g anchovies, well rinsed and finely chopped
1 large bunch of fresh parsley, leaves picked and finely chopped
100ml olive oil

Method
Mix all of the ingredients together.

MARINATED SHIITAKES

200g shiitakes or mushrooms of your choice
100ml olive oil
6 fresh sage leaves, finely sliced
juice of 1 unsprayed lemon
salt and freshly ground black pepper

Method

Sweat the mushrooms for 5 minutes in half the olive oil. Add the sage and sweat for a further 3–4 minutes. Add the lemon juice and the remaining olive oil, season to taste, then chill and refrigerate.

CHILLI AUBERGINES

2 large aubergines, peeled and cut into 10cm strips
1 small red chilli, seeded and finely chopped
100ml olive oil
juice of 1 unsprayed lemon
salt

Method

Mix all the ingredients together, then cook over a very gentle heat for 20 minutes, stirring occasionally. Add salt to taste, chill and reserve.

CORN SALSA

2 heads of corn, kernels well scraped off
4 tbsp olive oil
1 large shallot, peeled and chopped
juice of 1 unsprayed lime
salt and cayenne pepper

Method

Sweat the corn kernels very gently in the olive oil for 10 minutes over a medium heat, then add the chopped shallot and lime juice. Season with salt and cayenne.

BRAISED RED PEPPERS

2 large red peppers, seeded and cut into approx. 2cm strips
100ml olive oil
1 garlic clove, peeled and halved
1 large sprig of fresh oregano, leaves picked and finely chopped
salt

Method

Place the peppers, olive oil and garlic together in a pan, cover and braise for 15 minutes over a medium heat.

When cooked add the oregano and a little salt if necessary, then store in the oil until needed.

CHICKPEA PURÉE

You could, of course, cook your own chickpeas (see page 43), but using tinned is quicker. Serve with pitta bread, roasted vegetables or a selection of *crudités*. This purée, similar to hummus, also makes a great garnish for fish or poultry.

1 x 400g tin cooked chickpeas, rinsed
juice of 1 or 2 unsprayed lemons
2 garlic cloves, peeled
150ml olive oil

Method

In a blender, liquidise the chickpeas with a little water, the lemon juice, garlic and olive oil. You can blend the purée to the texture that you prefer: if you want it thinner add a little water. You can have it coarse or very fine.

TOMATO SALSA WITH ARTICHOKES

This lends itself to all sorts of different dishes. It's great with oily fish such as mackerel (see page 200), salmon, tuna, herring and sardines. But simply mixed with some mozzarella or feta cheese, it makes a wonderful lunchtime salad.

SERVES 4

Planning ahead
May be prepared a day in advance. This is nice since it allows the flavours to mingle, but is totally optional.

5 large, very ripe plum tomatoes, cored and roughly chopped
1 large red onion, peeled and finely chopped
100ml extra virgin olive oil
grated zest and juice of 1 unsprayed lime
1 small bunch of fresh coriander (parsley or basil), leaves picked and
 finely chopped
salt and freshly ground black pepper
a little dried chilli, crumbled (optional)
6 large bottled artichoke hearts, drained and cut in half

Method
Mix together the tomato, red onion, olive oil, lime zest and juice and your chosen herb. Then, depending on your personal preference, season with salt and black pepper or salt and dried chilli (if using). Add the halved artichokes and stir to combine.

DIPS

These dips may be served with a selection of *crudités* such as fennel, carrots and peppers, along with a little pitta bread where they will provide a light evening meal or lunch.

AVOCADO DIP

1 ripe avocado, peeled and stoned
juice of 1 unsprayed lemon
1 small tomato, cored and cut into chunks
2 medium shallots, peeled and finely diced
50ml olive oil
salt and freshly ground black pepper

Method
Mash the avocado in a bowl with the back of a fork. Add the lemon juice straightaway, then the rest of the ingredients and season to taste. If you are wanting to store this for any length of time, squeeze a little more lemon over the top and cover with clingfilm directly on the surface otherwise it will oxidise.

PEANUT AND CORIANDER DIP

A great alternative to peanut butter for the kids. Get them to help out by shelling the nuts.

300g fresh peanuts, shelled
75ml extra virgin olive oil
a few sprigs of fresh coriander, leaves picked and sliced

Method
Blend everything together in the food processor. If you prefer it chunky stop halfway through; if not, blend until smooth.

MAYONNAISE

Nutritional note
Many people are concerned about using raw egg yolks because of the risk of salmonella. However, there is less danger of infection in birds which are organically reared and free-range, because they are *fit*; they are well able, because of their own immunity, to contend with invading organisms. Vinegar or garlic used with raw egg can help protect against infectious agents.

2 large free-range egg yolks
1 tbsp Dijon mustard
1 tbsp hot water
150ml groundnut or sunflower oil

Method

Mix the egg yolks in a bowl together with the mustard and hot water. Pour in the oil in a slow steady stream, whisking continuously. Do not reserve in the fridge or the oil will harden and the mayonnaise will separate.

Variation

To make a garlic mayonnaise, mix 2 peeled garlic cloves, crushed with a little salt, with the egg yolks, mustard and hot water. Add extra virgin olive oil instead of the groundnut or sunflower oil.

ROASTED PEPPER MAYONNAISE

1 small red pepper
1 mild red chilli
2 large free-range egg yolks
1 garlic clove, peeled and crushed with a little salt
1 tbsp Dijon mustard
150ml extra virgin olive oil

Method

Roast the pepper and chilli over an open flame, the pepper for about 10 minutes, and the chilli for about 2, until the skins are charred. Transfer them to a bowl and cover with clingfilm for about 10 minutes. Remove them from the bowl, then skin and seed both. Either chop finely or purée then add to the egg yolks, garlic and mustard. Whisk in the oil in a slow steady stream, as above. (This mayonnaise can also be used to thicken a fish soup.)

SANDWICHES

A simple and complete food that can be transformed into whatever you like.
Good bread is vital.

BLUE CHEESE ON TOAST WITH PEARS AND WATERCRESS

This is a great way of using up any bits of blue cheese that you may have in
the fridge.

Nutritional note

The moulds which have been added to, and developed in, blue cheeses such as Roquefort and Stilton, not only provide good flavour, but also help to stimulate the lining of the gastrointestinal tract to produce good levels of antibodies.

SERVES I

100g Roquefort or Stilton cheese, crumbled
2 tbsp crème fraîche
1 wholemeal walnut and raisin roll, cut in half, or 1 slice of walnut bread
1 bunch of watercress, leaves picked and washed
1 small pear, cored and sliced

Method

Preheat your grill to its highest setting.

Mix half of the cheese with the *crème fraîche* and set aside. Toast the two
halves of roll on the outer sides only. Spread the blue cheese–*crème fraîche*
mixture across the untoasted sides. Place under your grill for 2–3 minutes until
the mixture begins to brown and bubble.

Mix the watercress with the sliced pear, and crumble the remainder of the
blue cheese into it. Top with the grilled blue cheese toasts.

PITTA BREAD WITH BACON AND SPINACH

SERVES 1

3 rashers of back bacon
1 tbsp grain mustard
1 tbsp white wine vinegar
5 tbsp olive oil
$^1/_2$ avocado, peeled, stoned and cut into chunks
50g spinach, washed and shredded
1 large wholemeal pitta bread

Method

Grill the rashers of bacon then cut into chunks. Mix the mustard together with the white wine vinegar and olive oil. Add the bacon, avocado and spinach to this, mix well, then stuff it all into the pitta bread which you have warmed up.

AUBERGINE AND RICOTTA SANDWICH WITH GRILLED TOMATOES

SERVES I

1 small aubergine
100g ricotta cheese
5 fresh basil leaves, shredded
1 very large, ripe plum tomato, cored
50ml olive oil
salt
1 slice *pain de campagne*

Method

Preheat your grill to its highest setting.

Place the aubergine underneath the grill for about 10 minutes, turning it occasionally until the skin has blackened. Remove and discard the skin and chop the flesh roughly. Mix this with the ricotta and basil and set aside.

Cut the tomato into four wedges and put in a pan with the olive oil and a little salt. Place under the grill for 5 minutes until the tomato begins to blacken slightly.

Toast the slice of *pain de campagne*, spread it with the ricotta and aubergine mixture, and top with the tomato and the olive oil in which it was cooked.

PITTA BREAD WITH CHICKPEA PURÉE AND ALFALFA

SERVES I

1 wholemeal pitta bread
½ recipe *Chickpea Purée* (see page 78, or a small tub of hummus from a
   deli)
1 punnet of alfalfa sprouts
1 small bunch of watercress or rocket, chopped
1 large ripe tomato, cored and sliced
salt and freshly ground black pepper

Method

Warm the pitta bread through and slice it into half through the middle
horizontally. Mix the chickpea purée with the alfalfa and watercress and spread
across one-half of the pitta. Top with the sliced tomato, seasoning it with salt
and pepper. Cover with the second half of the pitta bread and eat immediately.

CHICKEN AND AVOCADO SANDWICH

When rushing home from work, buy a free-range chicken breast, an avocado and a bunch of rocket, the rest you should have at home. You then have a meal in 10 minutes.

SERVES I

1 free-range chicken breast, skin on, approx. 180g, cut into 5 slices at an
   angle
2 tbsp olive oil
juice of 1 unsprayed lemon
salt and freshly ground black pepper
1 ripe avocado
1 shallot, peeled and diced (optional)
1 slice wholemeal *pain de campagne*, toasted
a handful of salad leaves

Method

Mix the sliced chicken with the olive oil and half the lemon juice. Heat a small frying pan, season the chicken pieces and fry them for 3–4 minutes on each side.

While this is cooking, skin, halve and stone the avocado. Cut one half into four. Squash the other half in a small bowl with the shallot and remaining lemon juice. Season the purée to taste and spread across the slice of toasted *pain de campagne.*

Top with the salad leaves, chicken breast and sliced avocado, give a good grind of pepper, relax and enjoy.

SOUPS

I suppose today that most people associate soups with a can rather than a delightful amalgam of fresh ingredients. In my childhood, our main meal was at midday, and a soup of the season or month's most abundant vegetable, with some salad and cheese, was often the evening meal.

For the most part, the soups in this chapter are very quick to make, and do not require too much in the way of forward-planning or shopping. Most are vegetable based, but some have a small protein element. When making a vegetable soup, stock need not be used; water is often better, allowing the true flavours of the vegetables and herbs to come through. When finishing with a fragrant soft-leaved herb such as basil or chervil, add it at the very last moment to ensure maximum freshness.

Soups represent comfort food to me, warm, filling and nourishing, but they can also play a major part in our diet. If you decide to make your own soups, it will not only be immeasurably healthier than opening a tin, but richly satisfying.

Soups can be served as a light meal by themselves, or as part of a meal, with perhaps one or two courses to follow. If served with bread, and perhaps followed by fruit and yogurt, they would make a good light, but healthy meal, especially for children. And they should be followed in a meal by dishes containing complementary nutrients.

When primarily made from vegetables, as here, they are a good source of carbohydrate and fibre; many of the principal ingredients, such as red pepper and butternut squash, are also rich sources of carotenoids (see page 14) and other nutrients. Occasionally, the soups have added protein, either from the addition of a stock, rich with the nutrients of a chicken carcass, or from the addition of seafood, which also contains good essential fats. Soups are good and healthy food.

JM

RB

JERUSALEM ARTICHOKE SOUP

SERVES 4

Planning ahead
This soup may be made completely in advance and reheated.

750g Jerusalem artichokes, peeled and chopped
1 large onion, peeled and finely chopped
2 tsp groundnut oil
200ml milk
salt and freshly ground black pepper

Method
Sweat the onion for 5 minutes in the groundnut oil. Add the Jerusalem artichokes and milk. Cover with water then boil for 15 minutes, topping up if necessary with more water.

When cooked, the artichokes should be totally soft (this saves you from having to pass them through a sieve). Liquidise in a blender until totally fine. Add a little more milk if the soup is too thick, and season to taste. Serve.

If you desire, a little chopped parsley or chervil would make a nice addition.

LEEK AND CHERVIL SOUP

SERVES 4

4 large leeks, with just the very tops of the green removed
40g unsalted butter
1 medium bunch of fresh chervil, leaves picked
salt and freshly ground black pepper

Method
The best and easiest way of preparing leeks for a recipe such as this is to cut them lengthways, without actually going through the root itself. Do this about six times and give the leeks a good wash. Then all you need to do is turn the leeks and cut them widthways into squares of about 2cm.

Once this is done, place the leeks with the butter into a large pan with a lid and sweat them for 10 minutes, being very careful that they do not colour. Add enough water to cover them, bring to the boil, then boil for 5 minutes.

Check to see if the leeks are totally soft, then add the chervil, some salt and plenty of black pepper, and serve.

VEGETABLE SOUP WITH BASIL

SERVES 4

2 medium onions, peeled, quartered and sliced
1 large fennel bulb, cut in sixths and sliced
1 large carrot, peeled, cut into quarters and sliced
4 garlic cloves, peeled and finely chopped
4 tbsp olive oil
4 large plum tomatoes, cored and diced
$^{1}/_{2}$ recipe *Basil Purée* (see page 38)
salt and freshly ground black pepper

Method
Once you have prepared the soup vegetables and garlic (you can do all of this
in the food processor), sweat them with the olive oil without colouring for
5 minutes. Cover with water and cook at a rapid boil for 10 minutes until the
vegetables are soft.

Add the tomato and basil purée, and season with salt and black pepper.

Variations
Almost any vegetable in season can be added to this soup, and you may add fresh
basil instead of the purée, or fresh chervil or parsley.

You can easily make a meal out of this soup by adding cooked wholemeal rice
or pasta, bulgar wheat or cooked flageolet beans.

TOMATO AND ROAST PEPPER SOUP

SERVES 4

Planning ahead
The soup may be made half a day in advance and reheated.

8 very ripe plum tomatoes, cored and coarsely chopped
4 large red peppers, seeded and coarsely chopped
50ml groundnut oil
approx. 200ml water
100ml extra virgin olive oil
salt and freshly ground black pepper

Method
Heat your largest pan with the groundnut oil. Add the tomato and red pepper and cook for approximately 5 minutes until they start to caramelise slightly. Remove from the heat and liquidise in a blender, adding enough water to achieve a soup-like consistency.

Whisk in the olive oil, then season with salt and pepper. Serve.

If you so desire, you could garnish the soup with a little fresh basil.

RB's note
Personally I enjoy a fairly chunky texture, and the skins and seeds that make it so hold a lot of vital nutrients, but if you prefer a smooth soup just pass it through a fine sieve.

CHILLED TURNIP AND ROCKET SOUP

SERVES 4

Planning ahead
This soup may be made a full day in advance.

500g young turnips, peeled and diced
150g (2 large bunches) rocket, quickly washed
3 tbsp groundnut oil
salt and freshly ground black pepper

Method
In a deep saucepan gently heat the groundnut oil, add the diced turnip and cover. Sweat this over a low heat for 5 minutes. Cover with water, bring to the boil then cook as quickly as possible, topping up the water level whenever necessary, for 20 minutes.

Add the rocket, stalks and all, and boil for a further 2 minutes.

Blend in a liquidiser until completely fine, then strain through a conical sieve and cool immediately over ice. If the soup is too thick, just add water. Season to taste and set aside until cold.

Pour the soup into four bowls and serve.

CURRIED CREAM OF CAULIFLOWER SOUP WITH CORIANDER PURÉE

SERVES 4

Planning ahead
As this soup may be served hot or cold, you can make it a day or so in advance. Make the coriander purée at the last moment or it will discolour.

1 large cauliflower, cut into small florets
1 small onion, peeled and coarsely chopped
1 tsp curry powder
2 tbsp groundnut oil
200ml whipping cream or milk
salt and freshly ground black pepper

THE CORIANDER PURÉE
1 small bunch of fresh coriander
50ml groundnut oil
juice of $1/2$ lemon

TO SERVE
2 tbsp groundnut oil mixed with $1/4$ tsp curry powder
1 tbsp coriander seeds, lightly crushed if you like

Method

The soup
Sweat the chopped onion with the curry powder in the groundnut oil for 2 minutes, then add the cauliflower florets and cook over a medium heat for 3 minutes. Cover with water and boil for 10–12 minutes until the cauliflower is totally soft. Add water if necessary during the cooking time to keep the cauliflower covered.

Add the cream and liquidise everything in a blender until smooth. Season well and set aside.

The coriander purée
Purée the coriander, leaves *and* stalks, oil and lemon juice together in a mortar and pestle or small blender, then season to taste.

Serving
Heat the soup gently, then pour into bowls and spoon over the coriander purée and curry oil. Sprinkle with the coriander seeds and serve.

RB's notes

The curry powder is sweated with the onions to help release its various spicy flavours. This must not be done at too high a temperature or it will burn and impart a bitter flavour.

The cream in the soup may be replaced by either bio yogurt or coconut milk. Do not boil these, as they can separate.

COCONUT AND LIME LEAF SOUP

SERVES 4

Planning ahead

This soup may be made totally in advance and reheated.

   1 x 6cm piece of fresh root ginger, peeled and finely chopped
   4 garlic cloves, peeled and finely chopped
   1 small green chilli, seeded and finely chopped
   1 large onion, peeled and sliced
   4 lemongrass stalks, coarsely chopped
   4 tbsp groundnut oil
   2 tins (approx. 800ml) unsweetened coconut milk
   400ml water
   4 fresh lime leaves, sliced
   juice of 2 unsprayed limes
   salt and cayenne pepper

Method

In a deep saucepan sweat the ginger, garlic, chilli, onion and lemongrass in the groundnut oil without colouring for 5 minutes. Pour over the coconut milk and the water and bring to the boil. Simmer for 10 minutes, then add the sliced lime leaves, and simmer for a further 5 minutes.

Strain through a fine sieve, add the lime juice and season to taste with salt and cayenne pepper. Serve.

Variations

This soup can easily be turned into a refreshing main course with the addition of some mussels, scallops and a little fresh coriander or, if you prefer, some chicken and some sliced carrots and leeks.

BUTTERNUT SQUASH AND LEMON SOUP

This recipe is a delicate mixture of the slightly sweet and acidic, and depends totally on the ripeness and quality of your squash.

Nutritional note

This is a good dish for children. The squash provides a rich source of beta-carotene; the onion adds flavour and, nutritionally, protective sulphur-containing compounds. The use of unsprayed lemons protects against the intrusion into the diet of waxes and other unnecessary components; and using the zest and juice in this way will add bioflavonoids and Vitamin C.

SERVES 4

Planning ahead
This soup may be made a day or so in advance and reheated.

1 butternut squash, approx. 1kg, peeled, seeded and cut into 3cm chunks
1 onion, peeled and sliced
2 tbsp groundnut oil
salt and freshly ground black pepper
grated zest and juice of 2 unsprayed lemons

Method
Sweat the squash and onion in the groundnut oil for 5 minutes. Cover with water, bring to the boil, and boil as quickly as possible for 10 minutes, topping up the water as necessary, until the squash is totally soft.

Pour into a blender and liquidise until completely smooth. Season to taste, add the lemon zest and juice, and serve.

CRAB CHOWDER

SERVES 4

250g cooked crabmeat
1 large onion, peeled and cut into 2–3cm dice
2 large carrots, peeled and cut into 2–3cm dice
1 large fennel bulb, cut into 2–3cm dice
2 large potatoes, peeled and cut into 2–3cm dice
45g butter
500ml milk or coconut milk
500ml water
cayenne pepper
1 small bunch of fresh parsley, leaves picked and sliced

Method

Sweat the vegetables in the butter in a saucepan for 5 minutes, then add the milk and water. Simmer for 10 minutes until the vegetables have softened.

Add the crab, bring the soup back to the boil and season with plenty of cayenne; as the crab is naturally quite salty, you should not need to add any salt.

Serve topped with the chopped parsley.

Variations

If you are brave enough, you could buy a couple of whole crabs and prepare them yourself. This way you could make a little stock from the shells and add it instead of the water. (The claws themselves are very decorative, and make a good addition to the soup.) This is, however, a lot of work and these days it is possible to get very good crabmeat (which is about 70 per cent white and 30 per cent brown meat) from quality supermarkets and delicatessens.

If you like a lean towards the Mediterranean, you could add a little saffron to this soup or, for an Asian influence, some chopped ginger and lemongrass, finishing with coriander instead of parsley.

ALMOND AND GARLIC SOUP

SERVES 4

Planning ahead
The soup may be made completely in advance and reheated.

    100g whole shelled almonds, coarsely chopped
    2 large heads of new-season garlic
    4 tbsp olive oil
    1 litre *White Chicken Stock* (see page 35)
    salt and freshly ground black pepper

Method
Preheat the oven to 180°C/350°F/Gas 4.

Spread the almonds on a baking sheet and toast for 10 minutes in the oven.

Peel the cloves of garlic and blanch them for 5 minutes in plenty of boiling water. Drain and dry.

Heat the olive oil in a saucepan, add the garlic and sauté for 3 minutes until golden. Add the almonds, pour over the chicken stock and bring to the boil. Skim well, then simmer for 5 minutes. Season to taste and serve.

Variations
Either cashews or hazelnuts could replace the almonds.

SOUP OF SUGAR-SNAP PEAS WITH BROAD BEANS AND LOVAGE

You can probably only make this soup if you grow broad beans and lovage in your own garden, but you can vary it (see below).

SERVES 4

800ml water
50g shallots, peeled and finely diced
50ml extra virgin olive oil
500g sugar-snap peas, topped, tailed and finely chopped
200g young broad beans in their pods, chopped
10 fresh lovage leaves, finely sliced (optional)
salt and freshly ground black pepper

Method
Bring the water to the boil.

In a saucepan, sweat the shallot in the olive oil over a gentle heat for 2–3 minutes. Add the chopped sugar-snaps and broad bean pods, cover with the boiling water, and boil for 5 minutes. Add the lovage.

Liquidise, strain, and season with salt and pepper. Serve immediately.

Variations
Mange tout, French beans, broccoli or peas could also be used.

This soup can also be served cold; put it on ice as soon as it comes out of the liquidiser so it retains its colour and flavour.

CLAM AND VEGETABLE SOUP

SERVES 4

Planning ahead
The stock and vegetables may be made a day or so in advance but the clams must be added just at the last moment to ensure their freshness.

48 small clams (*palourdes*), well rinsed
4 garlic cloves, peeled and crushed
2 small dried chillies, crumbled
1 small leek, washed and cut into thin slices
1 large onion, peeled and thinly sliced
1 large carrot, cut in 4 lengthways and sliced
1 large red pepper, seeded and diced
4 tbsp olive oil
about 1 litre water
1 small bunch of fresh parsley or basil, leaves picked and finely cut

Method
Sweat the garlic, chilli and vegetables in the olive oil for 3 minutes, then pour in the water. Simmer for 10 minutes until the vegetables are soft.

Add the clams and boil as quickly as possible until they open. About 3 minutes is usually sufficient; discard any that do not open. Sprinkle over the herbs and serve.

RB's note
Adding the clams at the last minute and cooking them as quickly as possible ensures that you will capture their full flavour.

CHICKEN AND SOY BROTH

Nutritional note

Chicken is an excellent source of protein. The soy sauce not only adds flavour, but, as it is extracted from soya beans, is helpful for women in regulating and counteracting menopausal symptoms (soya contains naturally occurring oestrogen). The ginger, garlic and lemongrass are all Superfoods (see Appendix).

SERVES 4

Planning ahead

Ask your butcher to chop the carcass or winglets for you as this is a bit of a messy job in a home kitchen. So long as the broth is kept well refrigerated it may be made the day before and reheated.

> the carcass and trimmings of 1 large chicken or about 1kg chicken winglets, roughly chopped
> 75ml soy sauce
> 1 x 3cm piece of fresh root ginger, unpeeled and finely chopped
> 3 garlic cloves, unpeeled and finely chopped
> 1 lemongrass stalk, sliced

Method

Place all of the ingredients into a pan that just holds them, cover with water and bring to the boil as quickly as possible. A lot of scum will rise to the surface; remove all of this with the aid of a ladle. Allow the broth to simmer over a medium heat, skimming as and when necessary, for half an hour.

Strain the broth through a fine sieve or chinois and serve piping hot.

Variations

This recipe is totally versatile, and can be made with fish or duck bones or the leftovers from your roast chicken or turkey.

If you want to turn the broth into a simple meal, you could add some cooked brown rice or soba noodles and vegetables, or you could make the *Asian Pot-au-feu* on page 246.

CURRIED MUSSEL AND VEGETABLE SOUP

SERVES 4

Planning ahead

The soup may be made a day in advance up to the point of adding the mussels and cream.

    36 mussels, well washed and bearded
    1 large carrot, peeled and cut into small cubes
    1 fennel bulb, cut into small cubes
    1 onion, peeled and cut into small cubes
    1 tsp curry powder
    4 tbsp groundnut oil
    100ml whipping cream (optional)
    salt and freshly ground black pepper

Method

In a deep saucepan sweat the vegetables and curry powder in the groundnut oil for 10 minutes without colouring, until the vegetables are almost totally soft.

Add enough water to just cover them, then boil rapidly for 5 minutes, topping up the water if necessary. Add the mussels and boil until they open; discard any that don't. Add the cream, heat through gently, then taste and season if necessary.

Serve either in individual bowls or a large tureen.

Variations

This soup is intended as either a starter or a lunchtime main course, but with the addition of a few potatoes, a little fish or a few more mussels, it can easily become a meal in itself.

SALADS AND STARTERS

This is a very general heading as I realise that three-course meals are not today's norm. Most of the starters here could become light lunches or suppers by increasing the ingredients slightly, or by accompanying them with one of the salads or a dressed green salad. Likewise the salads could be starters or partners for simply cooked fish or meats. By offering a mixture of them in slightly smaller quantities, they could be served as an *antipasto* or as part of a barbecue or buffet. Most are quick to prepare, and all are packed with delicious and healthy ingredients.

Feel free as always to experiment; if parsley fails to please you, use chervil; if mackerel is not to your taste, substitute sardines. The recipes are a base from which you can explore.

RB

For full enjoyment of food and for proper digestion to take place, we must be hungry. Usually hunger occurs only when the level of glucose stores are low and the stomach is empty. Some people, particularly obese people, overeat, but the body's appetite should be regulated by the senses of smell and taste. The smell and look of food increase the flow of saliva and start the digestive juices working – the beginnings of digestion.

The flavour of food must be appetising as well, of course, and there are many delicious ingredients here which will delight – but not sate – at the beginning of a meal. That many salads are included is healthy, for raw foods are excellent at stimulating metabolic function before a meal. The dressings of salads are useful in digestion as well: the vinegars and citrus juices which help to emulsify oils in these dressings, also contain acids which assist in the breakdown in the stomach of protein.

JM

CHICKEN LIVERS WITH RAW BEETROOT AND PORT VINAIGRETTE

SERVES 4

12 large organic chicken livers, all traces of sinew and gall bladder
removed
2 tbsp groundnut oil
salt and freshly ground black pepper
1 small bunch of fresh chervil, leaves picked, with the stalks

THE VINAIGRETTE
3 medium raw beetroot, peeled and grated
200ml ruby port, reduced to 50ml
2 tbsp red wine vinegar
2 tbsp water
50ml groundnut oil
50ml walnut oil
50g pine kernels

Method
First make the beetroot vinaigrette. Mix the reduced port with the vinegar and
water, and whisk in the groundnut and walnut oils. Add the grated beetroot and
pine kernels, then season to taste.

Heat a small frying pan with the groundnut oil. Season the livers then sauté
them for $1^1/_2$ minutes on each side. Remove from the pan and allow to rest for
a minute.

Serve the livers on top of the beetroot, sprinkled with the chervil.

CLASSIC POTATO SALAD

SERVES 4

Planning ahead
This salad may be made a while in advance, but is best served warm and must never be served cold.

800g small Ratte or Jersey potatoes
salt and freshly ground black pepper
1 bunch of fresh parsley, leaves picked and finely chopped

THE VINAIGRETTE
3–4 large shallots, approx. 120g, peeled and finely chopped
1½ tbsp water
3 tbsp white wine vinegar
100g groundnut oil

Method
Scrub your potatoes but do not peel them. Cook them at just under simmering point in plenty of salted water for 20 minutes or until soft.

While they are cooking prepare the vinaigrette. In a bowl that will be large enough to hold the potatoes, mix the shallot with the water and white wine vinegar, add the groundnut oil and season well.

Once they are cooked, drain the potatoes. Cut them into chunky pieces if necessary and mix while still warm with the vinaigrette.

Add the parsley, season to taste and eat as soon as possible.

Variations
This salad is wonderful on its own, but is equally good as an accompaniment for herring or duck *confit*.

Clockwise from top left:
Haricot bean, cherry tomato and basil salad; Classic potato salad; Beetroot and watercress salad, using rocket

HARICOT BEAN, CHERRY TOMATO AND BASIL SALAD

SERVES 4

Planning ahead

The salad is fine made half a day in advance, so long as you add the leaves and basil at the last minute, otherwise they blacken and lose their flavour. It can be served slightly warm if you like, but if not make sure that it is at least at room temperature so that you get the full flavour of the tomatoes.

250g dried haricot beans, freshly cooked (see page 43)
40 cherry tomatoes, cored and cut in half
100ml olive oil
grated zest and juice of 1 large unsprayed lemon
salt and freshly ground black pepper
2 small heads of radicchio, leaves picked and washed
1 bunch of fresh basil, leaves picked and shredded

Method

While the beans are still warm, strain off all the liquid and place them in a bowl. Add the halved cherry tomatoes, the olive oil, lemon juice and zest, then season well with salt and freshly ground black pepper.

Add the salad leaves and sliced basil, and toss well. Serve in glass bowls if you have them, with plenty of crusty wholemeal bread to mop up the olive oil and lemon.

RB's note

It is best to marinate the beans with the olive oil, lemon and tomatoes whilst they are still warm so that they soak up all of the flavours.

BEETROOT AND WATERCRESS SALAD

SERVES 4

Planning ahead

Feel free to make this salad well in advance, but don't serve it straight from the fridge or you won't get the benefit of its full flavour.

4 large beetroot, about 1kg in total, washed well
salt and freshly ground black pepper
100ml extra virgin olive oil
2 tbsp white wine vinegar
3 large shallots, peeled and finely chopped
1 very large bunch of watercress, leaves picked and roughly chopped

Method

Cook the beetroot in plenty of salted water until soft. This will generally take about an hour, but depends on the age of your beetroot. Once cooked, put on a pair of gloves and peel them.

Cut the flesh into small cubes and place in a bowl. Pour the olive oil and vinegar over while they are still hot so that they absorb all the flavours of both. Add the chopped shallot and the watercress, and mix well. Season to taste, then serve with a little Russian black bread.

Variation

Other greens can be used; why not try rocket?

SALAD OF MIXED SPROUTS WITH OLIVE OIL AND LEMON

Sprouted seeds, pulses and grains provide a wonderful mixture of texture and freshness. There are many varieties becoming available in supermarkets, or you can grow your own. Feel free to add a few handfuls of salad leaves or some cheese for a more substantial snack.

Nutritional note

When sprouted, seeds, grains and pulses contain many additional nutrients, particularly Vitamin C. The whole pumpkin seeds contain essential fatty acids, and the lemon juice contributes Vitamin C and bioflavonoids.

SERVES 4

800g mixed sprouts (alfalfa, bean, lentil, chickpea etc.)
4 tbsp pumpkin seeds
8 tbsp extra virgin olive oil
juice of 1 unsprayed lemon
salt and freshly ground black pepper

Method
Mix all of the ingredients together and season to taste.

SALAD OF MUSHROOMS AND ANCHOVIES

SERVES 4

500g very firm, very fresh, button mushrooms, well washed
juice of 1 unsprayed lemon
1 small bunch of fresh thyme, leaves picked
8 anchovy fillets, well rinsed and finely chopped
$^1/_2$ small mild chilli, seeded and finely chopped
100ml olive oil
80g Parmesan, finely grated
salt and freshly ground black pepper

Method

Slice the mushrooms about 5mm thick, then mix the slices with the lemon juice, thyme, anchovy and chilli. Add the olive oil and Parmesan, season to taste with salt and freshly ground black pepper and serve.

The mushrooms tend to give out a lot of juice, so have some good, crusty country bread to mop it up.

ASPARAGUS, CELERY AND LEEK SALAD

SERVES 4

16 asparagus spears, tough woody parts removed
white and pale green parts of 4 medium leeks, well washed and each cut
    into 4 at a slant
200g celery heart, sliced in long strips on a mandoline (if you don't have
    one just slice it as finely as possible with a knife)
salt

THE MARINADE
50ml white wine
3 tbsp sherry vinegar
1 tbsp coriander seeds, toasted for 1 minute
80ml extra virgin olive oil

TO SERVE
1/2 small bunch of fresh coriander, leaves picked

Method
First of all prepare the marinade. Bring the white wine and sherry vinegar to
the boil, boil for 1 minute then add the coriander seeds. Remove from the heat
then add the extra virgin olive oil. Set aside.

Bring a large pan of salted water to the boil, and blanch the leek for 10
minutes. Add the asparagus to the same water and cook for 3–4 minutes at a
rapid boil, then plunge into iced water to refresh. Mix the leek while still hot
with the marinade mixture. Add the sliced celery to the leek and set aside.

To serve, mix the asparagus with the leek, celery and marinade and divide
the mixture between four plates. Top with the picked coriander leaves and serve.

Variations
This is a delightful mixture but it is by no means set in stone. Almost any
combination of vegetables, cooked or raw as necessary, and marinated, hot or
cold, is lovely. Truly a salad for all seasons.

JERUSALEM ARTICHOKE AND CHERVIL SALAD

SERVES 4

800g Jerusalem artichokes, peeled and cut in 2.5–3cm pieces
salt and freshly ground black pepper
1 large bunch of fresh chervil, leaves picked

THE VINAIGRETTE
1 heaped tbsp Dijon mustard
3 tbsp white wine vinegar
1 tbsp water
100ml groundnut oil

Method
Cook the Jerusalem artichokes in plenty of salted water at just below simmering point for 10–15 minutes until soft but not breaking up.

Whilst they are cooking, mix the mustard, vinegar and water together in a bowl that will be large enough to hold the artichokes. Add the groundnut oil in a slow but steady stream, season to taste and set aside.

When the artichokes are cooked strain them into a colander then add them to the vinaigrette. As the artichokes at this stage are quite delicate, try to toss them rather than mixing with a spoon. Add the chervil, season a little more if necessary, and serve.

CEP AND MÂCHE SALAD WITH PARMESAN

This is a very special, extremely simple salad that you can make if you are lucky enough to find some small tight ceps during their relatively short season. Alternatively, you can substitute small, very white button mushrooms, or chestnut mushrooms.

SERVES 4

150g small very firm ceps, wiped but not washed
4 large handfuls of *mâche* (lamb's lettuce), well washed and dried
juice of 1 unsprayed lemon
80ml best extra virgin olive oil
sea salt and freshly ground black pepper
100g aged Parmesan, in shavings

Method

With a very sharp knife cut the ceps into slices about 3mm thick.

Mix the lemon juice with a spoonful of water and the olive oil. Season well.

Mix the *mâche* into the dressing first, followed by the Parmesan and, very delicately, the ceps. Serve lightly sprinkled with sea salt and black pepper.

BULGAR WHEAT AND CUCUMBER SALAD

SERVES 4

Planning ahead
The salad can easily be made a few hours before serving.

200g bulgar wheat
salt and freshly ground black pepper
100ml olive oil
juice of 2 unsprayed lemons
1 large red onion, peeled, halved and finely sliced
1 large English cucumber, halved lengthways, seeded and cut in slices at a
    slant
1 large bunch of fresh flat-leaf parsley, leaves picked and sliced

Method
Cook the bulgar wheat in plenty of boiling salted water for 10–12 minutes. Once cooked, strain it through a fine sieve and press well to remove any excess water.

Place it in a bowl and mix while still warm with the olive oil and lemon juice. Add the sliced onion, cucumber and parsley, season well to taste and serve.

Variations
Feel free to experiment with this one, the bulgar wheat is an excellent vehicle for many ideas. You could add a little cooked sliced chicken, some tomatoes and basil, cubes of feta cheese, some smoked salmon and gherkins, roasted peppers and their oil . . .

SALAD OF CELERIAC, POACHED EGG, LARDONS AND FRISÉE

SERVES 4

4 large free-range eggs, poached (see page 58)
salt and freshly ground black pepper

THE CELERIAC SALAD
350g celeriac, peeled and cut into fine *julienne* strips
100g streaky bacon, cut into *lardons*, blanched and refreshed
100ml groundnut oil
1 tbsp grain mustard
1 tbsp white wine vinegar
1 tbsp water

TO SERVE
1 small head of *frisée* (curly endive), leaves picked and washed
1 small bunch of fresh chives, finely sliced
2 slices wholemeal bread, cut into *croûtons* and toasted

Method

The poached eggs
Prepare a small bowl of iced water. Poach the eggs as described on page 58. With a slotted spoon transfer them to the iced water. Leave to cool completely, then set aside.

The celeriac salad
Fry the blanched *lardons* of bacon in 2 tbsp of the groundnut oil for 1 minute, empty them into a bowl and add the mustard, vinegar, water and remaining groundnut oil. Mix well and season with salt and pepper. Add the celeriac and mix well, season again and set aside to marinate for at least 2 hours.

Serving
Mix the celeriac, *frisée* and chives then serve on four plates topped with the poached eggs and *croûtons*.

Variations
The *frisée* can be replaced by a mix of batavia and cos lettuce or watercress. If you prefer, the poached eggs could be served hot.

CARPACCIO OF SEA BREAM WITH FLAVOURS OF THE ORIENT

Nutritional note

Raw fish needs to be as fresh and uncontaminated as possible, but is first-class protein and contains iodine, as does the seaweed. The raw vegetables provide carbohydrate, vitamins and minerals. The onions are naturally antibacterial and protective. The ginger aids digestion and provides flavour and other nutrients, as do the coriander, pumpkin seeds, lime zest and juice.

SERVES 4

4 x 65–75g fillets of royal sea bream, skinned
2 tbsp groundnut oil
salt and freshly ground white pepper
8 fresh coriander leaves, finely sliced
4 tbsp pumpkin seeds, toasted

THE VEGETABLE GARNISH

1 small carrot, peeled and cut into fine strips
1 small courgette, peeled and cut into fine strips
20g pickled ginger, cut into fine strips
1 tbsp fine *wakame* seaweed, soaked in warm water for 30 minutes, drained and rinsed
4 spring onions, finely sliced at a slant
grated zest and juice of 1 unsprayed lime
1 tbsp rice vinegar
40ml groundnut oil

Method

The fish

Slice each fillet of bream into 6 pieces at a slant. Brush a large piece of clingfilm with a little of the groundnut oil and sprinkle with salt and white pepper. Place the pieces from 1 bream fillet on to this in a round shape, pushing them together slightly. Brush them with more groundnut oil and sprinkle with salt and pepper. Top with another piece of clingfilm and, using a meat bat or cleaver, flatten the fish pieces until they are transparent. Repeat this with the remaining pieces of sea bream in three further and separate operations. Reserve in the fridge until needed.

The vegetable garnish and serving

Mix all the ingredients together and season well with salt and pepper.

Remove the top layer of clingfilm from each portion of sea bream. Place the sea bream flesh side down on the plates and peel off the second layer of clingfilm. Spread the vegetables across the top, sprinkle with coriander and pumpkin seeds, and serve.

EGG MAYONNAISE

SERVES 4

6 large free-range eggs
1 bunch of fresh watercress, leaves picked, or 1 handful of cos lettuce,
    leaves shredded
120g *Mayonnaise* (see page 81)
1 tsp snipped fresh chives

Method

Cover the eggs with water in a pan, bring to the boil then simmer gently for 10
minutes. Refresh under cold water then peel. Set aside.

Divide the watercress or shredded lettuce between four plates. Cut each egg
in half, arrange on the bed of salads and spoon the mayonnaise over. Sprinkle
with chives.

WHOLEMEAL PASTA WITH HAM AND GRUYÈRE CHEESE

SERVES 4

200g fresh wholemeal pasta
salt and freshly ground black pepper
2 tbsp extra virgin olive oil
100g cooked ham, finely chopped
200ml whipping cream
80g Gruyère cheese, grated
1 free-range egg yolk (optional)
1 tbsp fresh chopped parsley

Method

Bring a large pan of salted water to the boil. Add the pasta and boil rapidly for 8–10 minutes (or slightly less if you prefer it *al dente*). Strain through a colander and rinse under hot water to remove any excess starch.

In a frying pan gently heat the olive oil, add the ham and sauté for 1 minute, then add the cream and boil for 2 minutes to thicken it. Add the pasta and the Gruyère to the ham and cream, and stir. Cook for a further minute, covered. Mix in the egg yolk if using, and the parsley. Serve.

Variations

Finely sliced vegetables or mushrooms could be added to the pasta to give it more texture.

MARINATED SARDINES WITH CHICKPEAS

SERVES 4

Planning ahead
The sardines need to be marinated 12 or so hours in advance, and the chickpeas can either be bought cooked or freshly cooked a day or two before needed.

12 fillets of sardines
100ml olive oil
3 garlic cloves, peeled and crushed
salt and freshly ground black pepper
juice of 2 unsprayed lemons
1 small bunch of fresh fennel herb, chopped

THE CHICKPEAS
200g cooked chickpeas (see page 43), or 1 x 200g tin, well drained and
    rinsed
1 large red onion, peeled and finely chopped
1 small fennel bulb, finely sliced

Method

The fish
Heat the olive oil gently with the garlic and 1 tsp salt until simmering. Place the sardine fillets, skin side up, into a small tray in one layer, then pour the hot oil over along with the lemon juice. Leave to marinate in a cool place for 12 hours.

The chickpeas
Once cooked, strain the chickpeas from their liquid and mix with the onion and the fennel bulb. Set aside.

Serving
Strain the oil off the sardines and mix it with the chickpeas. Season to taste and spoon into four plates. Top these with the fillets of sardine, and sprinkle with the chopped fennel herb and plenty of black pepper. Serve.

GRILLED TUNA WITH AUBERGINE AND TOMATO CONFIT

SERVES 4

400g piece of tuna, rolled in clingfilm to make a sausage shape and
    sliced in 4
4 tbsp olive oil
rock salt and freshly ground black pepper
1 recipe *Tomato Confit* (see page 38)

THE AUBERGINE
1 small aubergine, topped and tailed then cut in 4 slices lengthways
50ml olive oil
2 tbsp balsamic vinegar

THE DRESSING
4 tbsp soured cream
juice of 1 unsprayed lemon
1 heaped tsp grain mustard
3 tbsp water
1 small bunch of fresh coriander, leaves picked and finely sliced

Method
Brush the tuna with the olive oil, and season well with salt and pepper. Heat a grill pan (or, if you don't have one, a frying pan) and grill the slices of tuna for 1$\frac{1}{2}$ minutes each side, turning the tuna 90 degrees after each 45 seconds to bar-mark it. Transfer to absorbent paper and set aside.

The aubergine
Heat the olive oil in a frying pan and fry the aubergine slices for 2 minutes each side, first over a very high heat then lowering the heat slightly. Once cooked, deglaze the pan with the balsamic vinegar and allow it to evaporate. Drain the aubergine on absorbent paper and set aside.

The dressing and serving
Mix all the dressing ingredients together, season to taste with salt and pepper, and reserve. Top the slices of aubergine with the tomato *confit*, followed by the tuna, and spoon the dressing around.

GRILLED TUNA AND AROMATIC VEGETABLES WITH OREGANO OIL

SERVES 4

240g tuna tail, cut into 20 slices 6cm long and 2cm thick
2 small courgettes, trimmed and each sliced into 6 on the bias
1 small aubergine, cut in half lengthways then each half cut in 6 slices
150g butternut squash, peeled and cut into slices 1cm thick
1 large red pepper, peeled, seeded and cut in 4 lengthways
juice of 1 unsprayed lemon
100ml olive oil
salt and freshly ground black pepper

THE OREGANO OIL
1 small bunch of fresh oregano, leaves picked
50ml olive oil
juice of $1/2$ unsprayed lemon

Method

The tuna and vegetables
Separately mix the tuna and each of the vegetables with a fifth of the olive oil. Season the tuna with salt and pepper.

Heat a grill pan until it reaches smoking point, and grill the tuna for 20 seconds on each side (it should be raw in the centre). Then grill the vegetables for $1^{1}/2$ seconds on each side. Put them all on a small tray, add the lemon juice and seasoning, then leave to marinate for at least 6 hours.

The oregano oil
In a small blender or mortar and pestle, blend the oregano leaves with the olive oil and lemon juice until you have a fine purée. Season well with salt and pepper and set aside.

Serving
On four oval plates arrange the butternut squash, the courgettes and the aubergines. Top these with the slices of tuna then cut each piece of pepper into three and lay these over the top. Spoon the oregano oil around and serve.

SAUTÉED SQUID WITH CHICKPEAS AND PAK-CHOI

This is a somewhat startling, delicious mixture, the first time I have ever used *pak-choi* raw. The texture and sweetness of it is in perfect contrast to the softness of the chickpeas and squid.

SERVES 4

Planning ahead
The vinaigrette may be made a day or so in advance. If you are cooking the chickpeas, they also may be done a day in advance.

400g cooked chickpeas (see page 43), or 1 x 400g tin, well drained and rinsed
2 medium squid, approx. 400g cleaned weight, cut into 3–4cm triangles or squares and lightly scored
4 tbsp olive oil
juice of 1 unsprayed lemon
1 head of *pak-choi*, stems sliced about 3cm thick, the leaves cut in 4cm pieces

THE VINAIGRETTE
2 large very ripe plum tomatoes, cored and chopped
1 x 3cm piece of fresh root ginger
1 small medium red chilli, seeded and finely chopped
2 tbsp white wine vinegar
2 tbsp water
100ml olive oil
salt and freshly ground black pepper

Method
In a non-stick pan sear the tomato, ginger and chilli for about 2 minutes until they start to caramelise, then add the vinegar and water and allow to evaporate slightly. Pour the tomato, chilli and vinegar mixture into the bowl of a blender or food processor and liquidise to a fine purée. While the mixer is still running, add the olive oil slowly as if making a mayonnaise. Season the mixture, transfer to a bowl, add the cooked chickpeas and set aside.

To finish the dish, heat a large frying pan with the olive oil, toss in the squid and sauté for 1½ minutes. Deglaze the pan with the lemon juice, and season. Serve the squid atop the chickpeas, tomato vinaigrette and *pak-choi*.

SOUSED MACKEREL WITH BEETROOT SALAD

SERVES 4

Planning ahead
The mackerel need to be marinated at least 12 hours in advance, and the beetroot salad is better prepared a day ahead of serving to merge the flavours.

4 small fillets of fresh mackerel
75ml each of white wine vinegar and white wine
150ml water
$\frac{1}{2}$ tsp salt
$\frac{1}{4}$ tsp fructose
6 black peppercorns, crushed
4 tbsp seasoned soured cream mixed with the juice of 1 lemon

THE BEETROOT SALAD
3 large beetroot, well washed
50ml groundnut oil
2 tbsp white wine vinegar
salt and freshly ground black pepper

Method

The fish
Check the mackerel fillets for scales that may have been left on. Lay the fillets flat on a small tray in one layer with the skin side facing up.

Bring the vinegar, wine, water, salt, fructose and black peppercorns to the boil. Leave to cool down slightly (about 30 seconds), then pour over the mackerel. Leave to marinate in a cool place for at least 12 hours.

The beetroot salad
Cook the beetroot in plenty of boiling salted water until totally soft (about 40–50 minutes). Then peel them and cut the flesh into dice. While still warm mix with the groundnut oil and vinegar, and season well with salt and pepper. Set aside.

Serving
This salad must be served at room temperature. Divide the dressed beetroot between four bowls. Spoon the soured cream around, and top the beetroot with the drained mackerel. Serve.

CRAB AND AVOCADO SALAD WITH COCONUT AND MINT

This recipe adds a little twist to the classic combination of crab and avocado. If you don't like the idea of the coconut, it would be equally lovely, albeit in a totally different way, with a lemon and olive oil dressing. If you are brave enough to prepare your own crabs, great, but there is now very good picked crabmeat available.

SERVES 4

Planning ahead
The coconut dressing may be made 12 or so hours in advance.

- 200g white crabmeat
- 2 large avocados
- 4 large handfuls of *mâche* (lamb's lettuce) or rocket, leaves picked and washed
- 8 fresh mint leaves, sliced
- 1 small mild red chilli, seeded and diced

THE DRESSING
- 50ml thick coconut cream
- juice of 1 unsprayed lime
- 100ml groundnut oil
- salt and freshly ground black pepper

Method
To make the dressing, mix the coconut cream with the lime juice, then add the oil, continually whisking as if you were making a mayonnaise. Season to taste and set aside.

Skin, halve and stone the avocados then cut each into 8 chunks. Mix these gently with all of the remaining ingredients plus the coconut dressing, and serve.

Variation
Leave out the crab and add a little extra avocado.

SMOKED SALMON WITH CREAMED ROCKET, CUCUMBER AND CHILLI

This makes a substantial starter or a light luncheon dish.

Nutritional note

Salmon is an oily fish, and will provide oil of the Omega-3 series, as well as protein. Rocket, cucumber and onion will add vegetable carbohydrate, vitamins and minerals. Chilli is a rich source of beta-carotene and, when added to a dish, even in small quantities, can be very valuable.

SERVES 4

400g cold smoked salmon, cut in 8 slices at a slant
1 large onion, peeled and finely chopped
50g butter
2 large bunches of rocket, leaves picked and washed
150ml whipping cream
$^{1}/_{2}$ English cucumber, seeded and finely diced
4 spring onions, sliced
1 fresh red chilli, seeded and finely chopped
freshly ground black pepper

Method

Sweat the chopped onion in 10g of the butter for 3–4 minutes until soft. Add the rocket and cream, and cook gently to wilt the rocket and reduce the cream by half.

In a separate pan, stir-fry the cucumber, spring onion and chilli in the remaining butter for 2 minutes without colour.

Divide the creamed rocket between four plates and top with the slices of smoked salmon. Sprinkle the cucumber, spring onion and chilli mixture over the top. Give a good grind of pepper, and serve.

OCTOPUS WITH GREEN BEANS, ONIONS AND FETA

Octopus is a bit of an acquired taste and texture, and you can now find it more readily. If not, you could use pan-fried squid or some marinated anchovies or sardines. Or indeed just eat the vegetables and feta without it.

SERVES 4

Planning ahead
The octopus may be cooked a couple of days in advance and kept refrigerated. In this case, marinate it in the olive oil and lemon juice.

400g octopus tentacles
salt and freshly ground black pepper
100ml extra virgin olive oil
juice of 2 unsprayed lemons
200g feta cheese, cut into cubes
2 large white onions, peeled and sliced as thinly as possible
400g green beans, topped, tailed, blanched for 2 minutes
24 black olives, halved and stoned
10 fresh mint leaves, thinly sliced

Method
Place the octopus in a pan with plenty of cold, lightly salted water, bring it to the boil and lower the heat. Cook at just below simmering point for $1^{1}/_{2}$–2 hours until tender. Strain through a colander then slice as thinly as possible while it is still as hot as you can handle.

Mix it first with the olive oil and lemon juice then add the remaining ingredients. Season well and serve.

CLAMS AND MUSSELS WITH LIME

SERVES 4

48 small mussels, bearded and rinsed
24 small clams, well rinsed
100ml white wine
80ml extra virgin olive oil
zest and juice of 1 unsprayed lime
2 large shallots, peeled and cut into 2cm dice
1 small carrot, peeled and cut into 2cm dice
1 small courgette, cut into 2cm dice
1 small fennel bulb, cut into 2cm dice
1 bunch of watercress, leaves picked and washed
salt and freshly ground black pepper

Method

Place the cleaned mussels and clams into a large pan and pour over the white wine. Cover and cook over the highest possible heat for about 5 minutes until they have all opened. Place a colander over the top of a bowl and pour the mussels and clams into this, shaking well to catch all of the cooking juices. Shell all the mussels and clams and set the flesh aside.

Strain the cooking juices into a saucepan and boil to reduce by half. Pour into a bowl and mix with the olive oil, lime zest and juice. Add the vegetables, watercress and shelled mussels and clams to this, season to taste and serve.

OYSTERS WITH SOURED CREAM AND RED WINE VINAIGRETTE

Nutritional note

Oysters are one of the richest sources of zinc, and here they provide the principal source of protein. Red wine when reduced in this way will lose its alcohol component, but will retain many other properties such as proanthocyanidins (see page 304). Watercress is rich in iron, Vitamin C and other minerals.

SERVES 4

Planning ahead

The vinaigrette may be made well in advance.

24 plump rock oysters in their shells
100ml thick soured cream or *crème fraîche*
1 small bunch of watercress, leaves picked and finely chopped (save a few whole for garnish)
salt and freshly ground black pepper

THE VINAIGRETTE

150ml red wine, reduced to 50ml
2 tbsp water
50ml groundnut oil
2 shallots, peeled and sliced as finely as possible

Method

To make the vinaigrette, mix the reduced red wine with the water, groundnut oil and the shallot; season to taste and set aside.

Mix the soured cream with the chopped watercress and season well with salt and freshly ground black pepper.

Open the oysters, and add their juices to the vinaigrette. Lift them out of their shells and set aside.

Half fill the shells with the soured cream–watercress mixture, place the oysters back on top, dress with the vinaigrette and reserved watercress leaves, and serve.

Variation

Eat the oysters with a squeeze of lemon juice.

RB's note

Get your fishmonger to open the oysters for you, if you are wary about doing it at home.

Although I can think of few experiences finer than taking oysters straight from the sea, opening and then swallowing them whole with their juices, I know that some are a little put off by the texture of raw oysters. If you would like to firm them up slightly poach them gently in their own juices for 10 seconds.

TIGER PRAWNS WITH FRESH MANGO AND ROCKET

SERVES 4

Planning ahead
The mango may be cooked a day in advance.

16 large tiger prawns, shelled and de-veined
1 large mango, ripe but firm, peeled, stoned and diced
4 shallots, peeled and finely chopped
3 tbsp red wine vinegar
1 tbsp fructose
3 tbsp groundnut oil
salt and freshly ground black pepper
1 large bunch of rocket or watercress, leaves picked and washed

Method
Place the mango dice in a small saucepan with the shallot, vinegar and fructose. Cook over a medium heat for about 5 minutes until most of the liquid has evaporated. Set aside.

Heat a large pan with the groundnut oil, season the prawns and sauté for 3 minutes until they start to change colour. Transfer from the pan to a warmed plate. Add the rocket leaves to the pan and stir well just until they wilt.

Spread the mango around the centres of four plates and top with the rocket and prawns. Serve immediately.

CHICKEN AND SNOWPEA SALAD

SERVES 4

Planning ahead
The chicken may be cooked and marinated well in advance, and the snowpeas can be blanched, refreshed and mixed with the other vegetables apart from the avocado 5–6 hours before serving.

4 x 150g free-range chicken breasts, skin removed
150g snowpeas, blanched and refreshed
1 small cucumber, seeded and sliced
1 bunch of spring onions, sliced
1 large avocado, peeled, stoned and cut in chunks (do this at the last
    moment)
salt and freshly ground black pepper

THE VINAIGRETTE
juice of 2 unsprayed lemons
2 tbsp water
100ml groundnut oil

Method
Heat a steamer and steam the chicken breasts over a medium heat for 12–14 minutes until cooked through.

While the chicken is cooking, make the vinaigrette by mixing the lemon juice with the water and whisking in the groundnut oil.

Once the chicken breasts are ready, transfer them directly to the vinaigrette and allow to marinate briefly.

Remove the breasts from the vinaigrette and slice each into three or four. Toss the vegetables in the vinaigrette, then season well to taste. Place into a large serving bowl, mix in the chicken slices, and serve.

RB's note
Marinating the chicken while it is still hot allows it to absorb the flavours of the vinaigrette.

If you like, the chicken could be served while still warm.

QUAIL WITH WARM CHILLI VINAIGRETTE

This salad may either be served as a dinner party starter or a light main course.

SERVES 4

4 free-range quails
200g French beans
200g podded broad beans
2 tbsp groundnut oil
salt and freshly ground black pepper
100g young podded peas

THE VINAIGRETTE

100ml white wine
2 tbsp white wine vinegar
1 small red onion, peeled and diced
1 mild red chilli, seeded and diced
50ml *Brown Chicken Stock* (see page 36)
50ml groundnut oil
2 tsp liquid honey

Method

Preheat your oven to 200°C/400°F/Gas 6.

First make the vinaigrette. Reduce the white wine and white wine vinegar with the diced red onion and chilli until almost completely evaporated, then add the stock and groundnut oil. Whisk in the honey, season to taste and set aside.

Separately, blanch the French beans and podded broad beans for 3–4 minutes each. Refresh in cold water, then drain well.

Heat an ovenproof pan with the groundnut oil and season the quails. Sear them for 3 minutes on each side then place in the preheated oven for a further 3. Allow to rest for at least 5 minutes then carve the breasts and legs from the carcass and roll them in the vinaigrette.

Mix the remainder of the vinaigrette with the beans and peas. Surround the quails with these on individual plates and serve.

RB's note

If you don't have any or don't want to make any you can omit the chicken stock and just add a little extra groundnut oil so that the vinaigrette is not too acid.

CHICKEN LIVER SALAD WITH LENTILS AND ORANGE

SERVES 4

Planning ahead
The lentils need to be cooked in advance, so they may be done up to 2 days beforehand and kept refrigerated.

250g fresh organic chicken livers, all traces of sinew and gall bladder removed
20ml groundnut oil
salt and freshly ground black pepper
1 large sprig of fresh rosemary, leaves picked and finely chopped

THE LENTILS
200g lentils, soaked for 2 hours
50g shallots, peeled and finely chopped
50g carrots, peeled and finely chopped
40ml groundnut oil
40ml walnut oil
grated zest of 2 unsprayed oranges
juice of 2 unsprayed oranges, boiled to reduce by two-thirds

THE FENNEL SALAD
100g fennel bulb, finely sliced lengthways
juice of $\frac{1}{2}$ unsprayed orange and $\frac{1}{2}$ unsprayed lemon
20ml groundnut oil

Method

The lentils

Drain the lentils then place in a large pan of cold water and bring them to the boil. Pour them into a colander and rinse well. Fill the pan with water again, and bring to the boil. Add the lentils, and simmer for 35 minutes (check that they are soft, this will depend on the type and age of the lentils), then drain. Keep warm.

While the lentils are cooking, cook the shallot and carrot in the groundnut oil for 5 minutes. Mix with the lentils, walnut oil, reduced orange juice and zest, and season well with salt and pepper. Set aside.

The fennel salad

Mix the sliced fennel with the juices and oil, then season well with salt and pepper and set aside.

The chicken livers and serving

Heat a frying pan with the groundnut oil, add the chicken livers and fry for 1 minute each side over a very high heat. Remove from the heat, season, add the rosemary and leave to rest for a further minute.

Distribute the lentils between four plates, top with the fennel salad and surround with the chicken livers.

Variation

The lentils could be replaced by kidney beans.

PAN-FRIED FOIE GRAS WITH WATERCRESS AND HAZELNUT SALAD

Nutritional note

Foie gras is an excellent source of protein and, like all offal, contains good quantities of vitamins, particularly the B complex. Using dandelion leaves here is good because they are likely to be fresh and organically grown, uncontaminated by pesticides. All seed and nut oils provide the Omega-3 essential fats. Watercress is a Superfood.

SERVES 4

4 x 100g slices of *foie gras*
salt and freshly ground black pepper

SALAD

1 bunch of fresh watercress leaves, picked and washed
1 small bunch of fresh dandelion leaves, picked and washed (optional)
2 tbsp sherry vinegar
2 tbsp water
30ml hazelnut oil
50ml groundnut oil
100g shelled hazelnuts

Method

Preheat the oven to 180°C/350°F/Gas 4.

Make the vinaigrette by mixing the sherry vinegar and water together. Add the oils and whisk in well. Season to taste and set aside.

Place the hazelnuts on a baking tray and roast in the oven for 10 minutes until golden brown. Set aside.

Get a frying pan extremely hot, season the *foie gras*, and pan-fry it for 1½ minutes on one side, 1 minute on the other; then place in the oven for 2 further minutes. Remove from the oven and allow to rest for at least 2 minutes.

Toss the salad leaves and roasted hazelnuts with the vinaigrette. Distribute this between four plates and top with the *foie gras*. Serve immediately.

PAN-FRIED FOIE GRAS WITH WILD MUSHROOMS AND ROCKET

SERVES 4

4 x 100g slices of *foie gras*
500g mixed wild mushrooms, trimmed and washed
20g butter
1 bunch of fresh rocket, washed and chopped
sea salt and freshly ground black pepper

Method

Preheat the oven to 180°C/350°F/Gas 4.

Sauté the mushrooms in the butter for about 4 minutes, depending on the variety. Add the rocket and season well. Keep warm.

Get a frying pan extremely hot, season the *foie gras*, and pan-fry for $1\frac{1}{2}$ minutes on one side, 1 minute on the other; then place in the oven for 2 further minutes. Remove from the oven and allow to rest for at least 2 minutes.

Serve the *foie gras* on top of the mushrooms and rocket, sprinkled with sea salt and freshly ground pepper.

PAN-FRIED FOIE GRAS WITH PEARS AND HONEY

SERVES 4

4 x 100g slices of *foie gras*
2 medium, ripe but firm Comice pears, each cored and cut into 6
25g unsalted butter
2 tbsp balsamic vinegar
2 tsp liquid honey
200ml *Brown Chicken Stock* (see page 36)
grated zest and juice of 1 unsprayed lime
salt and freshly ground black pepper

Method

Preheat the oven to 180°C/350°F/Gas 4.

Sauté the pear pieces in the butter for 2 minutes on each side. Deglaze the pan with the vinegar, and allow to evaporate completely. Add the honey and toss together until the honey melts and glazes the pears.

Remove the pears from the pan and add the chicken stock. Reduce by half then add the juice of the lime. Season to taste then add the cooked pears. Set aside.

Get a frying pan extremely hot, season the *foie gras* and pan-fry for $1\frac{1}{2}$ minutes on one side, 1 minute on the other; then place in the oven for 2 further minutes. Remove from the oven and allow to rest for at least 2 minutes.

During this time reheat the pears and sauce. Distribute the pears between four plates and top with the *foie gras*. Spoon the sauce over and sprinkle with the lime zest. Serve immediately.

RICOTTA AND SPINACH CROQUETTES

MAKES 8 CROQUETTES

100g spinach, leaves picked and washed
180g ricotta cheese
6 tbsp groundnut oil
60g Gruyère or Cheddar cheese, grated
salt and freshly ground black pepper
100g wholemeal flour
2 free-range eggs, beaten
150g wholemeal breadcrumbs

Method

Heat a pan with 2 tbsp of the groundnut oil, add the spinach, and fry for about 1$\frac{1}{2}$ minutes until it is totally wilted. Turn it into a colander and squeeze out all of the juices until the spinach is almost totally dry.

Chop the spinach into as small pieces as possible and mix it with the ricotta and grated Gruyère. Season to taste.

Rubbing a little wholemeal flour on your hands, make 8 little balls with the mixture; it will feel very soft, but this is how it should be. Roll these balls first in the wholemeal flour, then flatten them slightly. Dip them in the egg and then the breadcrumbs to coat well. Flatten them so that they look like mini burgers and fry them for 2 minutes each side in the remaining groundnut oil. Drain well and serve.

VEGETARIAN MAIN COURSES

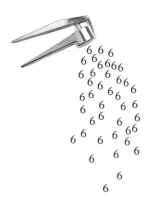

The days of a last-minute omelette or a large side-plate of vegetables as the choice for our vegetarian guests are long gone. I now have not only a vegetarian *à la carte* menu at Le Manoir, but also an eight-course sampling menu. I have had the same pleasure here in creating a range of dishes more suited to domestic cooking at home. It is not all limiting with the selection of fresh vegetables, grains, pulses and nuts that we now have at hand. To combine these with organic eggs or fresh or matured cheeses, provides a seemingly endless and tempting variety of full-flavoured and nutritious vegetarian dishes.

RB

Each of the dishes in this chapter has a variety of vegetable ingredients which together offer a wide range of vitamins, minerals and other nutrients. There are also a number of carbohydrate grains and pulses – among them polenta, brown rice, bulgar wheat and tofu – which, together with some vegetables, provide a good protein content. The tofu itself, made from soya beans, is as near to a complete protein as the vegetable world can supply. However, there is also protein in these dishes, supplied by a variety of cheeses, hard and soft, and by eggs, as well as nuts. Many of these dishes could actually serve as an accompaniment for meat dishes.

JM

BRAISED STUFFED WHITE ONIONS

SERVES 4

Planning ahead
This dish may be completely prepared a day in advance, although if this is the case, it will need to be reheated for 10–15 minutes before glazing.

> 4 large white onions, peeled
> 1 bay leaf
> 2 sprigs of fresh thyme
> 2 large garlic cloves, peeled and halved
> 150g Italian brown rice
> salt and freshly ground black pepper
> 50ml extra virgin olive oil
> 100g Parmesan, finely grated
> 1 bunch of fresh parsley, leaves picked and finely chopped
> 1 recipe chunky *Tomato Sauce* (see page 39)

Method

The onions
Bring a pan of water to the boil with the bay leaf, thyme and garlic. Add the onions and, if necessary, a little water to cover them completely, then bring back to the boil. Simmer over a medium heat for 1 hour, topping up with water as and when necessary until the onions are very soft.

The stuffing
Meanwhile boil the rice in plenty of salted water for 20–25 minutes until cooked. Strain it into a colander, ensuring that you remove all the liquid, then transfer to a bowl. Add the olive oil, half the grated Parmesan and half the chopped parsley; stir well to combine, season to taste, then set aside.

Once the onions are cooked, remove them from the water and let them cool. When able to handle them, cut each onion in half and remove the centres. Place these to one side, and stuff the remaining outer rings with the rice.

Finishing and serving
Pour the tomato sauce along with 2 ladles of the onion cooking liquor into the bottom of an ovenproof dish and gently place the stuffed onion halves on top of it. Surround with the onion centres.

Heat your grill to its highest setting. Sprinkle the remaining parsley over the top of the onions first, followed by the remaining Parmesan, and place under the grill until the dish is nicely glazed. Serve as is with a little salad on the side.

SUMMER SALAD OF TOMATOES AND GOAT'S CHEESE

SERVES 4

8 large, very ripe plum tomatoes, approx. 100g each, cored and thickly
   sliced
salt and freshly ground black pepper
10 black olives, stoned and halved
10 green olives, stoned and halved
100g French beans, topped, tailed and blanched
50g young podded broad beans (optional)
6 bottled artichoke hearts, halved lengthways
1 small fennel bulb, sliced as finely as possible
50ml olive oil
juice of $^1/_2$ unsprayed lemon
8 slices wholemeal *baguette*, cut at a slant and toasted on one side
4 tbsp *Basil Purée* (see page 38)
1 Sainte-Maure goat's cheese, cut into 8 slices

Method

Preheat the grill to its highest setting.

Season the sliced tomatoes and place them in a circle around the outside of
four plates. Scatter the olives, beans and artichokes around. Mix the sliced
fennel with the olive oil, lemon juice and a little salt and pepper, and pile this
in the centre.

Spread the untoasted side of the *baguette* slices with a little of the basil
purée, top with the goat's cheese and grill until the goat's cheese starts to
bubble and brown. Place on the sliced fennel. Spoon the remaining basil purée
around, and serve.

SPINACH, FETA CHEESE AND RED ONION GRATIN

SERVES 4

This dish makes a pleasant lunch with a little salad.

4 large red onions, peeled and finely sliced
2 tbsp groundnut oil
2 tbsp sherry vinegar or white wine vinegar
salt and freshly ground black pepper
400g feta cheese, cut into small cubes
2 large sprigs of fresh oregano, leaves picked and chopped
80ml olive oil
400g spinach, leaves picked, washed and dried
4 tbsp fine polenta

Method

Preheat the oven to 180°C/350°F/Gas 4.

Sweat the sliced red onion for 15 minutes in the groundnut oil until totally soft. Raise the heat and evaporate all the liquid, then add the sherry vinegar and allow to caramelise slightly. Season to taste and spread along the bottom of an ovenproof dish.

Mix the feta cheese with the oregano and 50ml of the olive oil and place over the top of the onions.

Toss the spinach in the remaining olive oil for about 2 minutes over a high heat until it wilts. Season well and spread over the top of the feta.

Sprinkle the polenta over the top in an even layer, bake in the oven for 10 minutes, and serve immediately.

POACHED EGGS WITH SPRING VEGETABLES

SERVES 4

8 large free-range eggs, poached (see page 58)
20 asparagus spears, trimmed
20 spring onions, trimmed
100g sugar-snap peas
1 large bunch of rocket, leaves picked and washed
1 large bunch of fresh chervil, leaves picked and washed
50ml olive oil
salt and freshly ground black pepper

Method

While the eggs are cooking, boil or steam the asparagus for 5 minutes, adding the spring onions and sugar-snaps after 2 minutes. Drain them and then place back into the pan. Add the rocket, chervil and olive oil, season to taste and keep warm.

To serve, remove the eggs from their cooking liquor with a slotted spoon, place on to four plates and top with the vegetables and herbs. Some cracked black pepper also makes a nice addition.

Variations

Any mixture of vegetables may be used. This is best in springtime so you will be absolutely spoiled for choice!

A few wholemeal garlic *croûtons* would make a pleasant addition.

PASTA WITH SWISS CHARD, GOAT'S CHEESE AND ARTICHOKES

SERVES 4

250g wholemeal pasta
salt and freshly ground black pepper
12 bottled artichoke hearts
1 small head of Swiss chard, stalks cut into 2cm pieces and blanched for
    2 minutes, the leaves coarsely shredded
4 tbsp olive oil
1 large bunch of rocket, stalks and all
300g fairly mature Sainte-Maure or other slightly crumbly goat's cheese
1 recipe *Rocket Purée* (see page 39)

Method

Boil the pasta in plenty of salted water for 8 minutes until *al dente*.

While this is cooking, sauté the artichoke hearts and the Swiss chard stems for 1 minute in the olive oil.

Strain the pasta and add it to the artichoke pan. Toss in the Swiss chard leaves and rocket, add the goat's cheese, stir in the rocket purée and serve.

RB's note

Swiss chard, for some reason, is quite hard to get hold of, and may be replaced by spinach or *pak-choi*.

FRIED BULGAR WHEAT PATTIES WITH MINT YOGURT

Nutritional note

The bulgar wheat provides a good source of carbohydrate and some protein. Complete protein is provided by the yogurt and pine kernels. Chilli, onion, garlic, mint and olive oil are all Superfoods (see Appendix). Aubergine, the principal vegetable here, is also a Superfood; the dark skin contains bioflavonoids, which reduce the risk of angina and strokes, and can lower cholesterol.

SERVES 4

Planning ahead
The pastry may be made, rolled and stuffed a few hours in advance.

1 recipe *Bulgar Wheat Pastry* (see page 42)
a little wholemeal flour

THE FILLING
1 medium onion, peeled and finely diced
1 small green chilli, seeded and finely chopped
3 garlic cloves, peeled and finely chopped
6 tbsp olive oil
200g mushrooms, washed and sliced
1 large aubergine, peeled and cut into strips
50g pine kernels
10 fresh mint leaves, chopped
salt and freshly ground black pepper

THE YOGURT
250g bio yogurt
8 fresh mint leaves, sliced
juice of 1 unsprayed lemon

TO FINISH
4 tbsp olive oil
a few handfuls of salad leaves such as rocket or curly endive

Method

The pastry

Make the pastry as described on page 42, and leave to rest for a while.

The filling

Sweat the onion, chilli and garlic in the olive oil for 5 minutes, then add the mushrooms, aubergine and pine kernels and raise the heat. Cook briskly, stirring frequently, for a further 5 minutes. Remove from the heat, add the chopped mint, season well and set aside.

The yogurt

Mix the ingredients together, and season to taste.

Assembling and serving

Dust a work surface with wholemeal flour, roll out the pastry and cut out 4 x 15cm diameter circles. Divide the filling mixture between these and fold one side over to enclose the filling and form a semi-circular shape. Seal the edges well.

Heat a frying pan with the olive oil and fry the patties for 3 minutes on each side until crisp. Serve with the salad leaves and the yogurt on the side.

GRILLED SHIITAKES WITH FLAGEOLET BEANS

SERVES 4

Planning ahead
If you are cooking the beans, do them a day or two in advance (see page 43).

28 large shiitake mushrooms
600g cooked flageolet beans (see page 43)
2 tbsp olive oil
2 large sprigs of fresh rosemary, leaves picked and chopped
salt and freshly ground black pepper

THE GARLIC EMULSION
2 large free-range eggs
2 garlic cloves, unpeeled
3 tbsp white wine vinegar
50ml extra virgin olive oil
50ml water

Method
For the garlic emulsion, boil the eggs with the garlic for 5 minutes. Skin the garlic and shell the eggs, then place them in the bowl of a blender or food processor with the vinegar and purée until fine. Add the oil in a slow steady stream while the motor is still running. Once it has emulsified add the water, and season to taste. Transfer to a bowl and mix with the cooked flageolet beans.

Heat a griddle or frying pan, mix the shiitakes with the olive oil, and grill or sauté for 3 minutes over a high heat. Add the rosemary and season well. Serve on top of the beans and garlic emulsion.

TIAN OF PROVENÇAL VEGETABLES

SERVES 2

Planning ahead
The entire dish may be made in advance and reheated.

2 onions, peeled and finely sliced
6 garlic cloves, peeled and sliced
3 tbsp olive oil
1 tsp salt
1 tsp fructose
1 aubergine, approx. 200g
1 large courgette, approx. 200g
2 large plum tomatoes, cored
4 sprigs of fresh thyme, leaves picked and chopped
20g wholemeal breadcrumbs
30g Parmesan, grated

Method
Preheat the oven to 150°C/300°F/Gas 2.

Sweat the onion and garlic together with the olive oil, salt and fructose for 10 minutes until soft. Raise the heat then, stirring constantly, cook for another 5 minutes until they begin to caramelise. Transfer them from the pan to an ovenproof dish and spread them flat across the bottom.

Cut the aubergine, courgette and tomatoes into 1.5cm slices. Season, and alternate the vegetable slices over the top of the onion mixture.

Sprinkle the thyme, breadcrumbs and Parmesan over the top, and bake for 1 hour in the preheated oven. Serve with a little salad dressed with olive oil and lemon.

BULGAR AND COURGETTE TART

SERVES 4

1 recipe *Bulgar Wheat Pastry* (see page 42)
a little wholemeal flour

THE TOPPING
300g ricotta cheese
2 tbsp Dijon mustard
salt and freshly ground black pepper
3 large courgettes, trimmed
3 tbsp olive oil
1 garlic clove, peeled and halved
20 black olives, halved and stoned
10 sun-dried tomatoes, chopped
4 tbsp capers, rinsed

Method
Preheat the oven to 180°C/350°F/Gas 4.

The pastry
Make the pastry as described on page 42, and leave to rest for a while.

Roll out the pastry with the aid of a little wholemeal flour and cut out 4 x 10cm diameter circles. Don't worry if they break a little, just push them back together. Place on a baking sheet and bake in the preheated oven for 8–10 minutes.

The topping
Meanwhile, mix the ricotta with the mustard, then season and set aside.

Slice the courgettes about 7–8mm thick. Heat a large frying pan with the olive oil and sauté the courgette slices with the halved garlic clove for about 2 minutes until softened but not coloured. Set aside on absorbent paper.

Mix the olives, sun-dried tomatoes and capers together and set aside.

Finishing and serving
Remove the tart bases from the oven and allow to cool. Spread them evenly with the mustardy ricotta. Circle the top with the courgettes, and finally sprinkle with the olive, sun-dried tomato and caper mixture. Bake for 5 minutes, and serve.

AUBERGINE ROLLED WITH ITS OWN CHUTNEY

This is one of my favourite dishes in the whole book. It comes from one of those experimental evenings when you introduce a number of friends from different paths and times of life that you are not sure will get on. But, magically, each one that arrives brings the others closer, and by the end no one can understand how they ever managed to be apart.

SERVES 4

Planning ahead
The whole dish may be assembled a full day in advance, ready to be reheated. If you are just making the chutney, it will keep for a good week in a sterilised jar.

2 large aubergines, approx. 350g each
juice of 2 unsprayed lemons
4 tbsp olive oil

THE CHUTNEY
the trimmings from the above aubergines (see method), cut into 4cm
    pieces
4 tbsp olive oil
100ml balsamic vinegar
150ml water
2 garlic cloves, peeled and crushed
1 small red chilli, seeded and finely chopped
2 tsp mustard seeds
2 tsp cumin seeds
1 tsp five-spice powder
100ml maple syrup
100g dried apricots, coarsely chopped
50g pine kernels

TO FINISH
100ml olive oil
juice of 1 unsprayed lemon
20 fresh mint leaves, sliced
150g feta cheese, cut into cubes

Method

Preheat the oven to 200°C/400°F/Gas 6.

Take 6 lengthways slices about 5mm thick from the centre of each aubergine. Cut the rest into dice for the chutney.

Place the slices of aubergine in a shallow tray and pour in the lemon juice and olive oil. Put in the preheated oven for 15 minutes to soften but not crisp. Remove and reserve.

To make the chutney, sauté the aubergine trimmings for 2 minutes in the olive oil, then add the rest of the chutney ingredients. Bring to the boil, cover, and simmer for 10 minutes. Remove the lid and simmer for a further 5 minutes. Set aside.

Divide this chutney mixture into two-thirds and one-third. With the two-thirds, mix the olive oil, the lemon juice and the mint. With the remaining third, mix the feta.

Lay the slices of aubergine flat on your work surface, divide the aubergine–feta mixture between them, and roll them up. You can then serve them either hot, cold or warm with the chutney, plus a little fresh green salad or some raw fennel on the side if you like.

ONION AND CEP TART WITH A POLENTA CRUST

This is a must, one of my very favourite recipes in this book.

SERVES 6

Planning ahead
The tart may be made half a day in advance and reheated.

THE POLENTA CRUST
150g polenta
300ml water
salt

THE FILLING
2 large onions, peeled and finely sliced
25g butter
50g dried ceps, soaked in 150ml warm water for 1 hour
250g mascarpone cheese
1 whole large free-range egg and 1 egg yolk
8 fresh sage leaves or 2 fresh sprigs of rosemary, leaves picked and finely
   chopped (optional)

Method
Preheat the oven to 160–180°C/325–350°F/Gas 3–4.

The polenta crust
Bring the water to the boil and slowly pour over the polenta and salt. Cook, stirring constantly over a medium heat, for 5 minutes. Remove from the heat and with the aid of a little more dry polenta, form into a ball.

Roll out as you would pastry, using polenta instead of flour to dust the work surface. Line a 20 x 2–2.5cm tart ring with it. Don't worry if it breaks up a little as you can push the pieces together to tidy it up. Prick the base then bake it in the preheated oven for 10 minutes. Then remove from the oven and turn the oven down to 160°C/325°F/Gas 3.

The filling
Sweat the onion in the butter without colouring for 5 minutes. Strain the ceps, keeping their liquor. Rinse the ceps gently and chop them coarsely. Add them to the onion and sweat for a further 2 minutes. Strain the cep juice on to this, and allow it to reduce completely. Transfer this mixture from the pan to a bowl and allow to cool.

Once cooled mix in the mascarpone, the egg, egg yolk and sage or rosemary if using. Spoon this mixture into the tart case, smooth it with a palette knife and cook for 20 minutes in the oven. Once cooked the tart should just tremble in the centre.

Serving

Serve in wedges hot, warm, or at room temperature. It would be lovely with the *Cep and Mâche Salad* on page 120 on the side, replacing the ceps with button mushrooms if fresh ceps are unavailable.

VEGETABLE AND CASHEW STIR-FRY

SERVES 4

Planning ahead

The vegetables may be all cut in advance and kept under a damp tea towel to be cooked at the last moment.

3 tbsp groundnut oil
2 large red peppers, seeded and cut into strips
1 large carrot, peeled and sliced
1 head of broccoli, cut into florets
1 head of *pak-choi*, finely sliced
150g beansprouts
100g cashew nuts
3 garlic cloves, peeled and finely chopped
1 x 3cm piece of fresh root ginger, peeled and finely chopped
1 small red chilli, seeded and diced
1 tbsp rice flour dissolved in 60ml dark soy sauce and 2 tbsp rice vinegar

Method

Heat the groundnut oil in a large wok or frying pan, add the pepper and carrot and stir-fry for 3 minutes. Add the broccoli, *pak-choi* and beansprouts then fry for a further 2 minutes. Toss in the cashews, garlic, ginger and chilli along with a few tablespoons of water and cook for a final minute. Pour in the dissolved rice flour and stir well to bind. Serve immediately.

ROASTED CEPS AND JERUSALEM ARTICHOKES

Although I imagine that it is of no interest whatsoever to a vegetarian, this is as close as one can come in texture to a meat dish using vegetables. The rich roasted flavour of the ceps and the slight sweetness of the Jerusalem artichokes is cut and enhanced by the light acidity of the shallot and red wine vinaigrette. The ceps may easily be replaced by shiitake mushrooms.

SERVES 4

20 small tight ceps, wiped and halved
20 Jerusalem artichokes, peeled and halved, blanched for 4–5 minutes
4 tbsp groundnut oil
40g unsalted butter
20 fresh flat-leaf parsley leaves, with their stalks

THE VINAIGRETTE
150ml red wine, reduced to 50ml
3 shallots, peeled and chopped as finely as possible
75ml olive oil
salt and freshly ground black pepper

Method
Preheat the oven to 180°C/350°F/Gas 4.

First make the vinaigrette. Mix all the ingredients together and season to taste.

Heat your largest frying pan with half the groundnut oil. Add the Jerusalem artichokes and fry over a high heat for about 4 minutes until they begin to turn golden brown. Transfer them to a tray lined with absorbent paper, and put them into the oven only while you prepare and cook the ceps.

Wipe out your pan and get it extremely hot again. Add the remaining groundnut oil and put in it the halved ceps. Fry for 2 minutes on each side until golden brown. Add the butter and parsley, leaves *and* stalks, and fry for a further minute.

Remove the artichokes from the oven, mix them with the ceps and parsley, and serve topped with the red wine vinaigrette.

RB's note
As the ceps have a very short season they may be replaced by frozen so long as they are totally defrosted and well dried beforehand.

TOFU 'LASAGNE'

Nutritional note

The soya-based tofu in this dish provides virtually complete protein, but it would be best eaten with some wholegrain bread. Ginger is warming and helpful to the digestion, and the sesame seeds add protein as well as essential fats. This dish is particularly useful for women, in that the soya in the *tofu* provides oestrogen-like components.

SERVES 4

Planning ahead
The 'lasagnes' may be made up in advance and then heated through in the sauce.

2 x 300g packets of firm *tofu*
4 large garlic cloves, peeled and finely chopped
1 x 6cm piece of fresh root ginger, peeled and finely chopped
4 large shallots, peeled and sliced
2 medium carrots, peeled and sliced
1 large head of *pak-choi*, leaves and stalks separated, and finely sliced
250ml soya milk
60ml thick dark soy sauce
10 leaves of fresh mint, finely sliced
4 sprigs of fresh coriander, finely sliced
1 small red chilli, seeded and finely chopped
4 tbsp sesame seeds
1 large bunch of watercress

Method

Preheat the oven to 180°C/350°F/Gas 4.

Slice each rectangle of *tofu* into 6, the full length of the rectangle, using a very sharp knife. Set aside on a tray.

Mix the chopped garlic and ginger together and place a third of this into a pan with the shallots and carrots; cover to the level of the carrots with water then boil for about 10 minutes until the water has all evaporated and the carrots are soft. Place into the bowl of your food processor and pulse to small chunks. Remove from the processor and set aside. Clean the bowl.

Stir-fry the *pak-choi* stalks for 2 minutes, then add the leaves and stir-fry for a further 2 minutes. Place these in the food processor and pulse to the same size as the carrots. Set aside.

Layer the *tofu* slices with first the carrots and then the *pak-choi*, finishing with a layer of *tofu*. Do this with the remaining *tofu*, carrot and *pak-choi*, to make 3 more lasagnes. Very carefully, using a fish slice, place them in an ovenproof dish and set aside.

Bring the soya milk to the boil with the soy sauce and the remaining garlic and ginger, then simmer to reduce by a third. Pour over the top of the *tofu* lasagnes. Place in the preheated oven for 10 minutes.

While the *tofu* is in the oven, mix the mint, coriander, chilli and sesame seeds together; steam the watercress to al dente. Serve the tofu surrounded by the watercress, the sauce and topped with the herb, chilli and sesame mixture.

Variation

Almost any mixture of vegetables may be used.

FISH AND SHELLFISH MAIN COURSES

In using fish and shellfish, the single most important point to remember is that they should all be as fresh as possible. If I get a wonderful shining mackerel still scented with the sea, I am quite happy to grill or bake it whole and serve it with lemon juice and a simple garnish. Mussels are delightful quickly cooked with a little white wine and a few shallots, and these can easily become a complete meal tossed with a little wholemeal pasta and a few sliced courgettes.

I have obviously included some recipes here that involve a little more work, but they are all, once again, open to your own interpretations and preferences.

RB

Fish and shellfish are good and healthy sources of protein, so long as they are fresh, from a reputable source, and uncontaminated (seafood can ingest metals such as mercury or other pollutants, all of which can be dangerous to humans). Fish and shellfish contain essential fatty acids, primarily of the Omega-3 series. In oily fish this fat is distributed through the flesh; in white fish, the fat is primarily in the liver (thus cod liver oil etc.). Seafood also contains many vitamins – A, D and the B complex – as well as iodine and calcium (in the soft bones which can be eaten, such as canned sardines or salmon).

JM

'GIGOT' OF MONKFISH WITH TOMATO AND PEPPER SAUCE

SERVES 4

A simple dish to prepare and serve, the flavours are wonderfully robust and true.

4 x 200g pieces of monkfish tail
6 garlic cloves, peeled and halved
salt and freshly ground black pepper
50ml olive oil

THE TOMATO AND PEPPER SAUCE

100ml olive oil
1 large onion, peeled and sliced
2 garlic cloves, peeled and sliced
2 large courgettes, trimmed, and sliced
2 red peppers, seeded and sliced
1 x 400g tin of tomatoes, roughly chopped, plus their juice
2 bay leaves
3 sprigs of fresh thyme
200ml water

Method

Preheat the oven to 180°C/350°F/Gas 4.

First prepare the monkfish. Make three small slits at regular intervals across the back of each piece of monkfish and insert 1 halved garlic clove into each slit. Set aside.

For the sauce, heat the oil, and sweat the sliced onion and garlic without colouring for about 3 minutes until they begin to soften. Add the courgette and pepper and sweat for 2 or 3 minutes more. Spoon in the chopped tinned tomatoes with their juices, herbs and water. Bring this to the boil, and simmer gently for about 5 minutes. Taste the sauce and season if necessary with salt and freshly ground black pepper.

Pour the sauce into an ovenproof dish, season the monkfish pieces and place them on top of it. Pour over the olive oil and place into the preheated oven. Allow to cook for 12–15 minutes, regularly basting with the sauce. Once cooked remove from the oven and allow to rest in a warm place for about 5 minutes. Serve in the cooking dish (see over).

BRILL IN TOMATO JUICE WITH CAPERS AND PARSLEY

SERVES 4

4 x 150g fillets of brill
40ml olive oil
1 large garlic clove, peeled and halved
8 small plum tomatoes, cored and cut in 4 lengthways
100ml white wine
1 tbsp salted capers, well rinsed
100ml water
4 large sprigs of fresh flat-leaf parsley, finely cut
salt and freshly ground black pepper
40ml extra virgin olive oil

Method

In a large frying pan heat the olive oil and fry the garlic clove until it is a dark brown colour. Add the tomato and sauté briskly for 1 minute. Pour over the white wine and reduce by half. Sprinkle over the capers.

Turn down the heat and place the fillets of fish on top. Pour in the water, braise for 5 minutes, then add the parsley, a little salt and a few turns of black pepper.

Distribute the tomato and juices between four deep plates, and top with the fish. Drizzle with extra virgin olive oil and serve.

TURBOT STEAKS WITH CHANTERELLES AND SPINACH

SERVES 4

Planning ahead
The sauce may be made a few hours in advance and reheated.

4 turbot steaks, each weighing 200g
25g unsalted butter
300g chanterelles, trimmed and washed
100ml white wine
150ml *Brown Chicken Stock* (see page 36)
3 tbsp groundnut oil
salt and freshly ground black pepper
400g spinach, leaves picked and washed

Method
Preheat the oven to 180°C/350°F/Gas 4.

Heat a saucepan with the butter, add the chanterelles and sweat for
2 minutes. Add the white wine and boil to reduce by two-thirds. Pour in the
stock, bring back to the boil, season to taste and set aside.

Heat an ovenproof frying pan with the oil, season the turbot well then fry
for 2 minutes each side until golden brown. Place in the oven for a further
4 minutes. Transfer to a warmed plate to rest.

Pour the fat from the pan and add the spinach. Sauté for 2–3 minutes until
softened, then season well.

Place the turbot back in the oven to heat it through, then serve on top of
the spinach covered with the mushrooms and sauce.

Variations
Steaks of halibut or cod would be equally good prepared this way. Any type of
mushroom may be used. If you like, a few fried sage leaves would be a nice
addition.

GRILLED SEA BASS WITH FENNEL AND LEMON

SERVES 4

4 pieces of sea bass fillet, weighing 180g each
4 large fennel bulbs, each cut in 6 lengthways
salt and freshly ground black pepper
100ml olive oil
juice of 1 unsprayed lemon
unsprayed lemon wedges, to serve

Method

Preheat your grill to a medium setting.

Boil or steam the fennel pieces for 5 minutes. Place them in the bottom of an ovenproof dish. Season the sea bass and place on top of the fennel. Pour over half the olive oil and all of the lemon juice. Place under the preheated grill and grill for 8 minutes. Transfer to plates and pour over the remainder of the olive oil. Serve with lemon wedges and a grind of black pepper.

Variations

Sea bream or red mullet could be used instead of the sea bass. A pleasant addition would be a few toasted fennel or onion seeds.

JOHN DORY WITH ARTICHOKES, CARROTS AND FENNEL

SERVES 4

John Dory has a wonderful flavour and texture that lends itself to very simple recipes such as this.

4 fillets of John Dory, each weighing approx. 160g
salt and freshly ground black pepper
2 x 300g fennel bulbs, trimmed and cut in quarters
12 large baby carrots, well washed
50ml light olive oil (or the oil from the artichokes)
4 large or 8 small bottled artichokes (preferably with stalks)
4 tbsp balsamic vinegar (as good a quality as possible)
2 large sprigs of fresh lemon thyme
50ml extra virgin olive oil

Method

The vegetables
Bring a large saucepan of salted water to a fast boil. Add the quartered fennel bulbs and boil for 2 minutes, then add the baby carrots and boil the two together for a further 4 minutes. Drain, and plunge them into iced water to refresh. As soon as they are chilled, remove from the iced water and set aside.

The fish
Preheat the oven to 180°C/350°F/Gas 4.
　　Heat an ovenproof sauté pan or small roasting tray with the light olive oil (or the oil from the artichokes). Add the vegetables, including the artichokes, and sauté for 1 minute.
　　Season the John Dory and place it in the pan with the vegetables. Fry over a high heat for 1 minute. Add 2 tbsp of the balsamic vinegar and the lemon thyme then place the pan in the oven for 4 minutes. Remove from the oven, turn the John Dory fillets over and allow to rest for 2 minutes in a warm place.

Serving
Place the John Dory fillets in the centres of four plates, surround with the vegetables, and spoon over the pan juices. Drizzle with the extra virgin olive oil and the remaining balsamic vinegar, and serve.

ROAST HALIBUT WITH ASPARAGUS, SPRING ONIONS AND SAGE OIL

SERVES 4

4 slices of halibut on the bone, each weighing 200g
salt and freshly ground black pepper
3 tbsp olive oil
20 asparagus spears, trimmed and halved widthways
12 spring onions, trimmed and halved widthways
12 *Tomato Confit* tomatoes (see page 38)
16 black olives, stoned and halved

THE SAGE OIL

8 fresh sage leaves, finely sliced
2 tbsp water
grated zest and juice of 1 unsprayed lemon
100ml olive oil

Method

Preheat the oven to 180°C/350°F/Gas 4.

For the sage oil, mix all the ingredients together and season well. Set aside.

Put a large pan of salted water on to boil.

Heat an ovenproof frying pan with the olive oil. Season the halibut well then fry for 2 minutes on each side until golden brown. Place in the oven for a further 4 minutes.

Meanwhile boil the asparagus for 3 minutes, adding the spring onions after 2. Once cooked *al dente*, remove them from the water and keep warm.

Remove the halibut from the oven, and place it on a tray in a warm place to rest.

Place the asparagus, spring onions, tomatoes and olives into the pan from which you have removed the halibut, add the sage oil, and heat through lightly. Season well.

Place the slices of halibut in the middle of four warmed plates, spoon the vegetables and sage oil over, and serve (see following page).

COD WITH CLAMS AND JERUSALEM ARTICHOKES

SERVES 4

Planning ahead

This dish involves three different pans and nothing can be prepared a long time in advance. However, the cod, the Jerusalem artichokes and the clams will all quite happily keep warm for 5–10 minutes, so it is a lot more simple than it seems.

4 slices of cod fillet, skin on, approx. 200g each
4 tbsp groundnut oil
salt and freshly ground black pepper
24 small clams, well rinsed
1 small bunch of fresh parsley, leaves picked and washed

THE JERUSALEM ARTICHOKES

500g Jerusalem artichokes, peeled and cut in slices about 1cm thick, well
    rinsed and dried
4 tbsp groundnut oil
40g unsalted butter

Method

Preheat the oven to 180°C/350°F/Gas 4.

Heat a large non-stick ovenproof frying pan with the groundnut oil. Season the pieces of cod well and place them in, skin side down. Fry over a medium heat for 5 minutes then place in the oven for a further 5 minutes. Once cooked, allow to rest in a warm place while you finish the other elements of the dish.

Heat another frying pan with oil for the artichokes, add the artichokes, and sauté over a high heat for 5 minutes. Add the butter and sauté for a further 6–7 minutes until the slices are well coloured and soft in the centre.

Place the clams into a saucepan with about 50ml water, cover tightly and cook as quickly as possible for 3 minutes until the clams all open. Discard any that don't. Add the parsley. Distribute the clams and their juices between four deep plates, top with the Jerusalem artichokes and cod, then serve.

STEAMED COD WITH WATERCRESS PURÉE

SERVES 4

Planning ahead
Both the watercress and potato purées may be made in advance. If this is the case, be sure to cool the watercress purée in a bowl over ice.

4 pieces of cod, each 180–200g
Mashed Potatoes (see page 210 and below)
salt and freshly ground black pepper
1 large bunch of watercress, bottoms of the stalks cut, well washed

Method
Heat a steamer, and bring another large pan of water to the boil. Make your mashed potato as on page 210, but omit the garlic, and use 30g butter instead of the hazelnut oil. Keep warm.

Season your cod and place it in the steamer for 6 minutes. Remove from the heat and keep warm.

While the cod is cooking drop the watercress into the boiling water and boil as rapidly as possible for 4 minutes. Lift the watercress out with a slotted spoon and purée with a little of the cooking liquor until fine. Season to taste, reheat a little if necessary then pour into four deep plates and top with first the potato and then the cod. Serve.

GRILLED TUNA WITH BORLOTTI BEANS AND SALSIFY

Salsify adds a lovely texture to this dish, but if you are unable to find it, just add a few more beans.

SERVES 4

Planning ahead
If you are cooking the beans, they may be cooked in advance as may the salsify.

4 x 170g pieces of tuna fillet
400g salsify, peeled, washed and cut into 3cm pieces
400g cooked borlotti beans (see page 43, or use tinned, drained and rinsed)
1 large red onion, peeled and coarsely chopped
50ml extra virgin olive oil
1 sprig of fresh rosemary, leaves picked and finely chopped
olive oil
salt and freshly ground black pepper
1 bunch of rocket, leaves picked and cut in half
unsprayed lemon wedges

Method
Blanch the salsify for 10 minutes in plenty of boiling water. Drain, then add to the beans and mix in the red onion, extra virgin olive oil and rosemary. Set aside.

Heat a grill pan or frying pan. Brush the tuna with a little olive oil, season with salt and pepper, then grill or fry for about 1½ minutes each side (less if you like it rare, a little more for medium).

Heat the bean mixture through, then add and stir in the rocket. When it wilts, divide the beans between four plates. Serve the tuna on top, with wedges of lemon and a grind of black pepper.

MONKFISH GLAZED WITH HONEY AND SOY SAUCE

SERVES 4

4 x 200g pieces of monkfish tail
400ml water
100ml soy sauce
2 tsp liquid honey
2 tbsp rice or white wine vinegar
1 small green chilli, seeded and finely chopped
2 tbsp sesame seeds
200g small shiitake mushrooms, stalked and washed
1 tsp cornflour, dissolved in 3 tbsp water
4 medium turnips, peeled and cut into 6 segments, blanched for
    4 minutes
150g soba noodles
salt
1 small bunch of fresh coriander, leaves picked and sliced

Method

Preheat the oven to 180°C/350°F/Gas 4.

Boil together the water, soy sauce, honey, rice vinegar, chopped chilli and sesame seeds. Add the shiitake mushrooms and allow to reduce by a third. Mix the dissolved cornflour in well, stirring constantly so that no lumps form.

Add the blanched turnip to this mixture, then pour into an ovenproof tray. Top with the pieces of monkfish and roll them around in the sauce. Place in the preheated oven and cook for 10–12 minutes, basting a few times with the sauce to give the monkfish a nice glaze.

While the fish is cooking, boil the soba noodles for about 5 minutes in plenty of salted water, then pour them into a colander and run hot water over the top for about 30 seconds. Place back into the saucepan with a little hot water and keep warm.

Once the monkfish is cooked, remove from the oven and allow to rest for a minute or two.

This dish is best served in deep plates or bowls. Divide the noodles between the centres of the plates and pour a little of the sauce over the top. Place a piece of monkfish in the middle of this, then spoon over the rest of the sauce, with the shiitakes and turnips. Sprinkle with the coriander, and serve.

Variations

This recipe would be excellent using any other firm-fleshed fish, or chicken or pork.

BRAISED SEA BREAM AND MUSSELS WITH SAFFRON POTATOES

A dish with the flavours of *bouillabaisse* but a lot less work!

Nutritional note

Sea bream and mussels are good sources of protein. Onion and garlic are Superfoods (see Appendix), providing sulphur components which will help in the digestion and metabolism of the protein. Saffron is helpful in providing minerals as well as colour. The potatoes are a good source of carbohydrate.

SERVES 4

Planning ahead

The saffron potatoes may be cooked in advance and reheated.

4 fillets of sea bream, skin on, pin-boned
24 small mussels, well washed and bearded
1 large onion, peeled and finely sliced
5 garlic cloves, peeled and finely sliced
1 sprig of fresh thyme
1 bay leaf
a healthy pinch of saffron strands
4 tbsp olive oil
4 large potatoes (King Edward or Roseval), peeled and cut in large cubes
freshly ground black pepper

Method

In a large flat pan with a lid, sweat the onion, garlic, thyme, bay leaf and saffron in the olive oil for 5 minutes without colouring.

Add the potato and sweat for a further 2 minutes. Pour in just enough water to cover the potato, and simmer very gently for approximately 10 minutes or until soft.

Add the mussels, replace the lid, then boil rapidly for about 2 minutes until they just begin to open. Discard any that don't.

Season the fillets of sea bream with pepper, then place them over the top of the potatoes and mussels. Cover the pan again, and allow to cook very gently for about 3 minutes. Serve in the pan for everyone to help themselves.

RB's note

As you are using mussels you should not need to add any salt.

Variations

This dish would work equally well with sea bass or red mullet. If you don't have any saffron, just add a little more thyme and bay leaf for a simpler but still very tasty alternative.

RED MULLET WITH GREEN OLIVE TAPENADE AND COURGETTES

SERVES 4

Planning ahead
The *tapenade* keeps well, so can be made in advance.

8 x 70g very fresh fillets of red mullet, skin on
salt and freshly ground black pepper
4 tbsp olive oil
3 medium courgettes, cut into 4mm thick slices
1 large bunch of rocket, leaves picked and chopped
2 garlic cloves, peeled and chopped
2 tbsp capers, well rinsed
1 recipe *Tapenade* made with green olives (see page 76)
1/2 bunch of fresh flat-leaf parsley, leaves picked and finely chopped

Method
Heat two frying pans. Spoon 2 tbsp of the olive oil into each of them. Into one, toss the courgettes, and into the other place the seasoned red mullet fillets, skin side down. Fry the red mullet for 2 minutes, then turn and fry for 30 seconds on the flesh side. Turn off the heat and allow to rest while you finish the courgettes.

Once the courgettes have been sautéed for 2 minutes, add the rocket, garlic and capers. Toss until the rocket has softened, then season to taste.

Mix the *tapenade* with the parsley and spread on half the mullet fillets. Serve one 'red' fillet and one 'green' fillet per person on top of the courgette and rocket mixture.

PAN-FRIED SEA BREAM WITH MARINATED VEGETABLES

SERVES 4

Planning ahead

The vegetables may be prepared in a food processor and are better marinated half a day in advance as they take on the flavours of each other. The olive oil and lemon juice will also serve to soften them slightly.

4 fillets of sea bream, skin on, pin-boned
2 tbsp olive oil
salt and freshly ground black pepper

THE VEGETABLES

1 small fennel bulb, trimmed and finely sliced
1 red onion, peeled and finely sliced
1 medium carrot, peeled and finely sliced
1 medium courgette, finely sliced
juice of 2 large unsprayed lemons
$\frac{1}{2}$ tsp fructose
200ml olive oil
1 small bunch of fresh coriander, leaves picked and finely sliced

Method

Mix all the vegetables together with the lemon juice and fructose, add salt to taste, then a little freshly ground black pepper. Leave this mixture to stand for half an hour at room temperature so that the vegetables begin to marinate, then add the olive oil and coriander. Check the seasoning then set aside.

Heat the 2 tbsp olive oil in a non-stick pan. Season the sea bream fillets and fry, flesh side down for 1 minute; turn gently then fry over a high heat for 2 minutes. Keep warm.

Place half of the vegetable mixture into the bottom of four large plates. Top with the fillets of sea bream then the remaining vegetable mixture. Serve.

Variations

This wonderfully fresh, simple recipe would lend itself well to sardines, mackerel, salmon – whatever your fishmonger has that is the freshest!

STEAMED SALMON AND PAK-CHOI WITH TABASCO OIL

SERVES 4

4 pieces of salmon fillet, each weighing 150g
2 heads of *pak-choi*
salt and freshly ground black pepper
80ml groundnut oil
juice of 2 unsprayed limes
2 tbsp Tabasco sauce
1 small bunch of fresh coriander, leaves picked and chopped

Method

Separate the leaves from the stalks of the *pak-choi*, and cut each stalk into 6–8 strips lengthways.

Heat your steamer and season the salmon and *pak-choi* stalks and leaves. Steam the salmon and *pak-choi* stalks for 5–6 minutes, then add the leaves and steam for a further minute.

Meanwhile, mix the groundnut oil with the lime juice, Tabasco and coriander. Season to taste and set aside.

Serve the salmon on top of the *pak-choi*. Stir the Tabasco oil well and pour it over and around.

Variations

This recipe would work very well with sea bass. If you have difficulty finding *pak-choi* it can be replaced by spring cabbage.

BAKED MACKEREL WITH ARTICHOKE AND TOMATO SALSA

SERVES 4

Planning ahead

The *salsa* may be prepared a day in advance.

8 fillets of mackerel, central bone line removed
salt and freshly ground black pepper
a little dried chilli, crumbled
100ml dry white wine
1 recipe *Tomato Salsa with Artichokes* (see page 79)

Method

Preheat the oven to 190°C/375°F/Gas 5.

Lay the mackerel fillets flat in a baking tray. Season and sprinkle with chilli and wine. Bake in the preheated oven for 6–7 minutes.

Spoon the *salsa* into four warmed plates and top with the mackerel fillets. If you feel like it, pour over a bit of extra olive oil and add a grind of black pepper. Serve.

Variations

The mackerel could be replaced by other oily fish such as salmon, tuna, herring or sardines.

PAN-FRIED SALMON WITH COURGETTES AND RADISH VINAIGRETTE

SERVES 4

Planning ahead

The marinated courgettes and radishes may be prepared a few hours in advance.

4 fillets of salmon, each weighing 150g
salt and freshly ground black pepper
200ml olive oil

THE VEGETABLES AND VINAIGRETTE

2 medium courgettes, cut into 3mm slices
10 radishes, cut into small dice
2 tsp white wine vinegar
4 large sage leaves, finely sliced

Method

Preheat the oven to 160°C/325°F/Gas 3.

Season the fillets of salmon well with salt and pepper, place in a pan that just holds them. Warm the olive oil slightly and cover the salmon with it. Place in the preheated oven for 8 minutes, then remove and leave to cool to room temperature in the oil. Set aside.

Mix the courgette and radish with 80ml of the salmon cooking oil, the vinegar and sliced sage, then add some salt and pepper. Put the courgette mixture around the centres of four plates, place the drained fillets of salmon on top, and spoon the remaining radish vinaigrette over.

RB's notes

The salmon is best served at room temperature, but may be served either warm or cold.

There is a lot of olive oil in this recipe which, on the face of it, makes it seem expensive, but this oil may be re-used, either in the same recipe again, or to make a salad dressing for a smoked salmon salad, or perhaps with a mixture of herbs and a little tomato *coulis* as a dressing for grilled salmon. I was brought up never to throw anything away, and now enjoy immensely the challenge of using up leftovers.

RED MULLET WITH TAHINI SAUCE AND CRAB COUSCOUS

SERVES 4

8 x 70g very fresh fillets of red mullet, skin on
salt and freshly ground black pepper
2 tbsp groundnut oil

THE COUSCOUS
120g couscous
120ml water
50ml extra virgin olive oil
200g cooked crabmeat, preferably two-thirds white, one-third brown
juice of 1 unsprayed lemon
12 fresh mint leaves, finely sliced

THE *TAHINI* SAUCE
4 heaped tbsp *tahini* (sesame paste)
1 garlic clove, peeled and crushed
50ml water
juice of 2 unsprayed lemons
50ml extra virgin olive oil

Method

The couscous
Boil the water then pour it over the top of the couscous in a bowl. Add the olive oil and cover. Leave for an hour until the couscous swells to about twice its original size. Set aside.

The *tahini* sauce
Mix all the ingredients together and season to taste. If necessary, add the juice of an extra lemon.

Finishing and serving
Heat the couscous and add the crab, lemon juice and mint. Season to taste and keep warm.

Season the red mullet and fry in the oil in a non-stick pan for about 2 minutes on the skin side, then turn the fillets. Gently fry for 30 seconds.

Spoon the sauce into four plates, then place the couscous in the centres. Top with the fillets of red mullet and serve.

TIGER PRAWNS, SMOKED AUBERGINE PURÉE AND RADICCHIO

SERVES 4

Planning ahead

The aubergine purée may be prepared a day or so in advance, and also makes an excellent dip.

20 tiger prawns, de-veined and washed
2 tbsp olive oil
2 small heads of radicchio, leaves picked and washed
salt and freshly ground black pepper

THE AUBERGINE PURÉE

2 aubergines, approx. 400g each
juice of 1 unsprayed lemon

THE SAUTÉED AUBERGINE

1 aubergine, approx. 400g, cut into 4 thick slices widthways
50ml olive oil
juice of 1 unsprayed lemon

Method

The aubergine purée

Place the aubergines over an open flame for 10 minutes, turning them four or five times until the skin is charred and blackened. Leave to cool slightly then peel off the skin, making sure that no trace of black remains. Purée the flesh with the lemon juice, season to taste, and set aside.

The sautéed aubergine

Heat a pan with the olive oil and cook the thick round aubergine slices for 3–4 minutes on each side until they are totally soft. Deglaze the pan with the lemon juice and set aside.

The prawns and serving

Heat the olive oil in a frying pan then season and add the prawns. Toss over a high heat for about 2 minutes until the prawns take on an orange-pink colour. Add the radicchio and toss just enough to warm it slightly.

Spoon the aubergine purée into the bases of four plates, top with the sautéed aubergine slices, the prawns and radicchio, and serve.

SARDINES WITH OLIVE TOMATO VINAIGRETTE AND CHICKPEA PURÉE

SERVES 4

Planning ahead
The chickpea purée may be made well in advance, or even bought.

20 fillets of sardine, as fresh as possible
salt and freshly ground black pepper
4 tbsp olive oil
1 recipe *Chickpea Purée* (see page 78)

THE VINAIGRETTE
100ml extra virgin olive oil
20 green olives, stoned and chopped
2 plum tomatoes, cored and chopped into cubes
juice of 1 unsprayed lemon
1 sprig of fresh rosemary, leaves picked and very finely chopped

Method
For the vinaigrette, mix all the ingredients together, and season to taste.

Preheat your grill to its highest setting.

Place the sardines, skin side up, on a tray and season them well. Spoon over the olive oil and grill for 3–4 minutes.

Spoon the chickpea purée into the centres of four plates, top with the sardines, and pour the vinaigrette over and around.

MACKEREL WITH A POTATO AND ROCKET SALAD

SERVES 4

Planning ahead

As it can be served either warm or at room temperature, you can make the potato and rocket salad in advance.

8 fillets of mackerel, central bone line removed
salt and freshly ground black pepper
100ml dry white wine

THE SALAD

800g new potatoes (Charlotte, Ratte or Roseval), unpeeled, well washed
2 large bunches of rocket, roughly shredded
1 tbsp grain mustard
2 tbsp white wine vinegar
2 tbsp water
3 tbsp soured cream
100ml groundnut oil

Method

The salad

Cook the potatoes in plenty of salted water at just below simmering point for 15–20 minutes until soft.

While they are cooking, take a bowl large enough to hold all the potatoes and mix in it the grain mustard with the vinegar, water and soured cream. Whisk in the groundnut oil to emulsify, then season to taste. Once the potatoes are cooked, drain them well and while they are still hot, mix them with the mustard dressing in the bowl. Add the rocket, stalks and all, to the potatoes, mix well and set aside.

The fish

Preheat the oven to 190°C/375°F/Gas 5. Lay the mackerel fillets flat in a baking tray. Season and sprinkle with the wine. Bake in the preheated oven for 6–7 minutes. Keep warm.

Serving

Divide the potato and rocket salad between four plates and top with the mackerel fillets. Grind a little black pepper over the top and serve.

CRAB CAKES WITH COURGETTE CHUTNEY

The polenta provides a marvellous crust and texture to the exterior of the crab cake, the flavours of which are set off by the sweet and sour of the courgette chutney. This could be a lunch main course or a substantial starter.

Nutritional note

The crabmeat and egg are excellent sources of protein. The polenta is a good source of carbohydrate, as are the brown breadcrumbs. Pumpkin seeds are the richest source of some of the essential fatty acids, particularly the Omega-6 series.

SERVES 4

Planning ahead
The chutney may be made a few days in advance, the crab cakes a good few hours before serving. All that you need to do at the last minute is dust the cakes with the polenta and fry.

THE CRAB CAKES
250g mixed white and brown crabmeat
80g fresh brown breadcrumbs
40g pumpkin seeds
1 whole free-range egg plus 1 egg yolk
10 fresh coriander leaves, shredded
salt and cayenne pepper
juice of 1 unsprayed lemon

THE CHUTNEY
3 medium courgettes, approx. 500g, cut into 2.5cm dice
100ml white wine vinegar
150g sultanas
1 small lemon, cut into 6 lengthways, then finely sliced
1 small hot chilli, seeded and diced
1 x 3cm piece of fresh root ginger, grated
5 tbsp liquid honey
30g pumpkin seeds

TO FINISH AND SERVE
4 heaped tbsp polenta
4 tbsp olive oil
unsprayed lemon wedges

Method

The crab cakes
Mix all of the ingredients together, seasoning well with salt, cayenne pepper and the lemon juice. Rub your hands with a little polenta if necessary and form four flat cakes. Set aside.

The chutney

Place all the ingredients, except for the courgettes, into a pan, cover and simmer for 20 minutes. Add the courgette pieces and simmer for a further 10 minutes, stirring frequently. Allow to cool.

Finishing and serving

Preheat the oven to 180°C/350°F/Gas 4.

Dust the tops and sides of the crab cakes with the polenta, and pat them lightly to ensure that they are well coated.

Heat a non-stick pan with the olive oil and fry the crab cakes over a medium heat for 2 minutes on each side. Place them in the oven for a further 3 minutes then remove. Serve on top of the courgette chutney, with lemon wedges.

MACKEREL WITH MASHED POTATOES AND HAZELNUT VINAIGRETTE

SERVES 4

8 fillets of mackerel, central bone line removed
salt and freshly ground black pepper
100ml dry white wine
2 bunches of watercress, washed and leaves picked

THE MASHED POTATOES
4 large floury potatoes, peeled and roughly chopped
6 large garlic cloves, peeled
100ml milk
40ml hazelnut oil

THE VINAIGRETTE
1 tsp Dijon mustard
1 tbsp white wine vinegar
2 tbsp water
40ml hazelnut oil
60ml groundnut oil
100g hazelnuts, toasted and roughly chopped

Method

The potatoes
Boil the potatoes and garlic together in plenty of lightly salted water for about 20 minutes until soft. Strain them into a colander. Meanwhile, heat the milk.

Mash the potatoes and garlic, using a large fork, or pass through a sieve. Stir in the hot milk, using a wooden spoon or spatula, not a whisk. Add the hazelnut oil and season to taste. Keep warm.

The vinaigrette
Whisk together the Dijon mustard, the wine vinegar and water, then add both the oils and whisk to emulsify. Stir in the chopped hazelnuts. Set aside.

The fish and serving

Preheat the oven to 190°C/375°F/Gas 5. Lay the mackerel fillets in a baking tray. Season and sprinkle with the wine. Bake in the preheated oven for 6–7 minutes. Remove the mackerel from the oven and keep warm.

Steam the watercress briefly. When it begins to wilt, place in a small pan, add the vinaigrette and warm through gently.

Spoon the mashed potato into the centres of four warmed plates, top with the mackerel fillets and finish with the watercress and vinaigrette.

RB's notes

When making the mashed potato it is important to use a floury type of potato as suggested, or the potato will become too elastic. For the same reason, use a wooden spoon, not a whisk, for stirring the potato.

SQUID, PARMESAN AND PARSLEY SALAD

SERVES 4

400g squid, cleaned and cut into fine strips
8 slices wholemeal bread, cut into 3cm *croûtons*
100ml extra virgin olive oil
1 small bunch of fresh parsley, leaves picked and finely chopped
50g Parmesan, grated
salt and freshly ground black pepper
1 head of radicchio, leaves picked and washed
4 good handfuls of *mâche* (lamb's lettuce), leaves picked and washed
2 tbsp white wine vinegar

Method

Preheat the oven to 200°C/400°F/Gas 6.

Scatter the *croûtons* on a baking tray and place them into the oven for 5 minutes until they are evenly golden.

Heat a frying pan with 3 tbsp of the olive oil, add the squid, and sauté over a brisk heat for 2 minutes. Add the *croûtons*, chopped parsley and finally the grated Parmesan, and toss well to combine.

Season to taste, then mix with the salad leaves in a large bowl. Add the remaining olive oil, the vinegar and a little more salt and pepper as necessary. Serve in the bowl, for everyone to help themselves.

BRAISED SQUID WITH RICE PILAFF

SERVES 4

Planning ahead
The tomato sauce and rice pilaff may be made a few hours in advance.

> 4 medium squid tubes, each weighing approx. 120g, well cleaned and washed
> 1 large onion, peeled and finely chopped
> 4 garlic cloves, peeled and chopped
> 4 tbsp olive oil
> 150g short-grain Italian brown rice
> 300ml water
> 1 bunch of fresh parsley, leaves picked and chopped
> 4 large sprigs of fresh oregano, leaves picked and chopped
> 1 recipe *Tomato Sauce* (see page 39)
> salt and freshly ground black pepper
> 60g ground almonds

Method
Preheat the oven to 200°C/400°F/Gas 6.

Sweat the onion and garlic in the olive oil for 3 minutes. Add the rice and sweat for a further 2, then pour in the water. Cook over a moderate heat, stirring occasionally, for 25–30 minutes until the rice has absorbed all of the water and is soft; you may need to add a little more water during the cooking time.

Mix half the parsley into the rice, along with the oregano, and season to taste. Stuff the rice mixture into the squid tubes, leaving a little room at the top to allow for the squid to shrink, then close the ends with skewers.

Pour the tomato sauce into an ovenproof dish then top with the squid tubes. Sprinkle with the ground almonds and the remaining parsley, then bake in the preheated oven for 15–20 minutes. Serve as is, with perhaps a little salad on the side.

TIGER PRAWN AND RADISH SPAGHETTI

SERVES 4

200g dried wholemeal spaghetti
salt and freshly ground black pepper
100ml olive oil
20 tiger prawns, peeled and de-veined
20 radishes and their leaves, each radish cut in 4 lengthways, the leaves
    left whole
3 garlic cloves, peeled and finely chopped
grated zest and juice of 2 unsprayed limes

Method

Bring a large pot of salted water to the boil and place the pasta on to cook, about 10–12 minutes. Be sure to taste, as brands differ.

Heat a large frying pan with the olive oil. Add the prawns and the radishes and sauté for 2 minutes. Add the garlic and sauté for a further minute until the prawns have taken on a wonderful pink colour and are completely cooked. Add the lime zest and juice and keep warm.

Once the pasta is cooked *al dente*, pour it into a colander and run hot water over the top of it for 30 seconds. Add the pasta to the prawn and radish mixture, along with the radish leaves, stirring with a pair of tongs so all is well incorporated without being broken up. Season well and serve in four warmed bowls.

RB's notes

Don't be surprised if the wholemeal pasta breaks up a little more quickly than the pastas you are used to; this is because it is unrefined. You'll be surprised at how good it tastes, I know I was!

Running hot water over the pasta once it is cooked ensures that you wash off the starch and don't end up with a plate of stodgy spaghetti that is all stuck together.

SALMON FISHCAKES WITH TOMATO SAUCE

Nutritional note

Salmon is one of the best sources of essential fats, and of course provides excellent protein, as does the egg. Peas will give a good contrasting texture and many nutrients. The tomato sauce contains many nutrients as well, but will also encourage children to enjoy the flavours of onion and garlic, and provide them with the essential fat of olive oil.

SERVES 4

320g salmon fillet
salt and freshly ground black pepper
a dash of lemon juice
100ml water
50g unsalted butter
300g floury potatoes
1 free-range egg
100g podded peas, cooked for 2 minutes and refreshed
2 tbsp wholemeal flour
2 free-range eggs, beaten
100g wholemeal breadcrumbs
50ml groundnut oil for frying
1 recipe chunky *Tomato Sauce* (see page 39)

Method

The fish cakes

Preheat the oven to 180°C/350°F/Gas 4. Season the salmon fillet with salt, pepper and lemon juice. Place in a small roasting tray with the water and 30g of the butter. Cover and cook in the preheated oven for 15 minutes. Remove and cool. Flake the salmon fillet.

Cook the potatoes in their skins in salted simmering water for 20–30 minutes, according to size. Remove, cool down for 10 minutes, then peel. Mash them with a fork and add the remaining butter. Mix in the salmon flakes, the egg and the cooked peas. Taste and correct seasoning. Allow to cool down.

Lightly flour your work surface. Divide the fish mixture into four and shape into fishcakes with your hands or a cutter. Coat them with flour, then dip them into the beaten egg and lastly coat them with breadcrumbs. Reserve.

Cooking and serving

Preheat the oven to 180°C/350°F/Gas 4.

In an ovenproof frying pan, heat the groundnut oil, add the fishcakes and fry for 2 minutes on each side. Place in the oven and heat through for a further 2 minutes.

While this is heating, warm the tomato sauce. Spoon this into the centres of four plates, top with the fishcakes, and serve.

PASTA WITH MUSSELS, COURGETTE AND CHILLI

SERVES 4

200g dried wholemeal spaghetti or fettucine
salt and freshly ground black pepper
100ml olive oil
2 large courgettes, finely sliced
3 garlic cloves, peeled and finely chopped
$\frac{1}{2}$ mild red chilli, seeded and finely chopped
48 mussels, well washed and bearded
100ml white wine
100ml water
1 small bunch of fresh oregano, leaves picked and finely chopped

Method

Bring a large pan of salted water to the boil and place the pasta on to cook.

Heat a deep frying pan with a lid with half the olive oil. Add the courgette, garlic and chilli and cook for 2 minutes without colouring. Add the mussels and white wine, boil to allow the wine to reduce by a third, then add the water. Cover the pan then cook as rapidly as possible for about 3 minutes until all the mussels open (discard any that don't). Keep warm.

Once the pasta is cooked *al dente*, pour it into a colander and run hot water over the top of it for 30 seconds. Add the pasta and oregano to the mussels and stir with a pair of tongs so that all is well incorporated without being broken up. Season well, and serve into four large warmed bowls.

RB's note

Any mussels that don't open should be discarded as they are potentially dangerous.

Variation

A more expensive but even more delicious version of this dish can be made with the wonderful little clams known as *palourdes*.

SCALLOPS WITH CHICKPEA CAKES AND YELLOW PEPPER VINAIGRETTE

SERVES 4

12 large fat scallops with their corals (roes)
3 tbsp olive oil
salt and freshly ground black pepper
1 large bunch of watercress, leaves picked and washed

THE VINAIGRETTE
1 large yellow pepper, seeded and cut into 3cm dice
100ml extra virgin olive oil
3 tbsp red wine vinegar
juice of 1 unsprayed lime

THE CHICKPEA CAKES
90g chickpea flour
250ml water
1 tbsp white mustard seeds
1 tbsp onion seeds
$^1/_2$ tbsp curry powder
10 fresh mint leaves, finely shredded

Method

The vinaigrette
Sweat the diced pepper in the olive oil over a low heat for about 5 minutes until soft. Transfer to a bowl, add the red wine vinegar and lime juice, season well and set aside.

The chickpea cakes
Bring the water to the boil with the seeds and curry powder. Slowly pour in the chickpea flour and stir continually over a medium heat for 15 minutes. It will thicken considerably, rather like polenta. Season well then divide the mixture into four. Shape into flat squares or circles.

Finishing and serving
Preheat the grill to its highest heat. Grill the chickpea cakes until golden brown on top. Season the scallops, and sauté for about $1^1/_2$ minutes on each side in the olive oil. Toss with the watercress and vinaigrette and serve on top of the grilled chickpea cakes, sprinkled with the mint.

SCALLOP AND SHIITAKE STIR-FRY

SERVES 4

12 large scallops and their corals (roes)
2 tbsp sesame oil
3 tbsp groundnut oil
200g shiitake mushrooms
2 heads of baby *pak-choi*, the leaves left whole, stalks sliced into 2cm
    pieces
40 sugar-snap peas, cut in half lengthways
1 x 3cm piece of fresh root ginger, peeled and finely chopped
2 garlic cloves, peeled and finely chopped
juice of 1 unsprayed lime
salt and freshly ground black pepper

Method

Cut each scallop in half and each coral into 3 pieces. Heat a large pan or wok with the two oils, add the scallops and corals, and toss for a minute over your highest heat. Add the shiitake mushrooms, sliced *pak-choi* stalks and sugar-snap peas, then sauté for a further minute.

Spoon in the ginger and garlic along with the *pak-choi* leaves and a little water, and stir-fry all together for another minute or 2 until the leaves have wilted. Add the lime juice, season to taste then serve on four large warmed plates.

RB's note

If you can't do without it, of course you may add a little soy sauce to your stir-fry. But there is such a wonderful mixture of the sweet and bitter, the soft and the crunchy, that I think you won't find it necessary.

Variations

Monkfish would make a wonderful substitute for the scallops, and if you can't find *pak-choi*, feel free to use Chinese cabbage, *choi-sum*, or spinach.

Likewise if shiitake mushrooms are not to your liking, any mushroom can be used instead.

ROASTED SCALLOP, ROCKET AND PARMESAN SALAD

SERVES 4

12 large scallops and their corals (roes)
2 tbsp groundnut oil
4 good handfuls of rocket, leaves picked, washed and dried
120g of the best Parmesan you can afford, sliced into shavings with a
    vegetable peeler

THE VINAIGRETTE

3 tbsp water
2 tbsp balsamic vinegar
salt and freshly ground black pepper
100ml olive oil
1 large shallot, peeled and finely chopped

Method

First make the vinaigrette. Mix together the water and balsamic vinegar with a little salt and pepper. Add the olive oil and shallot, then season to personal taste. Set aside.

Slice each scallop in half and each coral into 3 or 4 pieces. Heat a non-stick pan with the groundnut oil then place the scallops and corals into it. Fry them for 2 minutes on one side until they turn a lovely golden brown colour, then fry for a further 30 seconds on the other side. Turn off the heat and keep the scallops warm in the pan.

Mix the rocket with half the Parmesan shavings and the balsamic vinaigrette. Add the scallops, their corals and juices, then turn the salad a few times so that everything is well coated in the vinaigrette. Place in four large bowls, scatter with the remaining Parmesan, and serve.

PAN-FRIED OYSTERS WITH MUSHROOM PURÉE AND CHERVIL

Nutritional note

Oysters are a rich source of protein and zinc. Mushrooms will provide pantothenic acid, a B vitamin. The wholemeal bread is a source of carbohydrate and B vitamins. Garlic and onion are Superfoods (see Appendix).

SERVES 4

Planning ahead
The mushroom purée may be made 12 or so hours in advance and reheated.

24 large oysters (No. 2)
4 slices of wholemeal bread, cut into 1cm croûtons
50g butter
juice of 1 unsprayed lemon
6 sprigs of fresh chervil, leaves picked
salt and freshly ground black pepper

THE MUSHROOM PURÉE
300g button mushrooms, well washed
3 garlic cloves, peeled and finely chopped
1 large onion, peeled and finely chopped
25g butter
300ml milk
100ml whipping cream

Method

The mushroom purée
Sweat the garlic and onion in the butter for 5 minutes, then add the mushrooms and sweat for a further 3. Add the milk and cream, bring to the boil, simmer for 5 minutes then liquidise in a blender until totally smooth. Pour back into the pan and keep hot.

Finishing and serving
Preheat the oven to 180°C/350°F/Gas 4.
   Place the *croûtons* in a baking tray and bake in the oven for 5 or so minutes until golden brown. Set aside.
   Heat the butter in a frying pan until foaming and golden, add the oysters in a single layer and fry for 30 seconds on one side only. Add the lemon juice and chervil leaves and season well.
   Serve the oysters on top of the mushroom purée, coated with the cooking butter and chervil, and sprinkled with the *croûtons*.

MEAT, POULTRY AND GAME MAIN COURSES

If you always buy organic meat and game, and make sure that your poultry is free-range, you will quickly discern the superior tastes and textures. I've spoken and written many times before of the importance of professional butchers, and will once again stress this point. The meat you use needs to have care taken not only in its production but in the hanging and storing as well. To watch a proud butcher at work is for me a great pleasure as we are all part of a team and chain of quality, from the farmer in the fields to the cook in the kitchen.

My mother helped me out here, I must admit. I have used some of the recipes I enjoyed during my childhood, and these may take a little longer to cook, but are still actually very quick in the preparation. A minimum of stocks are used in the sauces: if you have a fine steak from organic beef, a lovely *jus* can be made simply by removing the fat from the pan and adding a few spoonfuls of water with which you scrape off the caramelised cooking juices. With a touch of salt and pepper, you have the meat's 'essence'.

'Meat' means the edible muscle of animals, principally of mammals such as cattle, sheep and pigs, and poultry such as chicken, turkey and duck. The offal is also eaten. Other meats are of game animals and birds – pheasants, partridges, rabbit and venison. All meat, whether red (beef, lamb, pork, venison) or white (poultry, rabbit) is rich in protein (which is more readily assimilated in the human body than vegetable protein), as well as iron, zinc and the B vitamins. Offal contains Vitamins A, B and D.

All meats contain saturated fat, the red meats in particular, so helpings should not be too lavish, or too frequent. Game would make a good alternative as it is less fatty than farmed meat, and often game birds and animals have enjoyed a natural and pure diet.

JM

RB

ROASTED BEST END OF LAMB

SERVES 4

Planning ahead
The vinaigrette may be prepared a day in advance, and if you are cooking your own chickpeas, these may also be done a day or two beforehand (see page 43).

2 large best ends of lamb, French trimmed (ask your butcher to do this
 for you)
2 tbsp groundnut oil
salt and freshly ground black pepper
200g cooked chickpeas, well drained and patted dry (see page 43)
100g pine kernels
2 large sprigs of fresh rosemary, leaves picked and finely chopped
200g young spinach, leaves picked, washed and shredded

THE EMULSION
50g pine kernels
2 tbsp water
1 tbsp white wine vinegar
60ml groundnut oil

Method
Preheat the oven to 200°C/400°F/Gas 6.

The lamb
Heat a large ovenproof pan with the groundnut oil. Season then sear the lamb, flesh side down for 1½–2 minutes until well browned. Drain the fat off. Turn the meat on to the fat side, then add the chickpeas and pine kernels to the pan. Cook in the preheated oven for 12–14 minutes, stirring the chickpeas and pine kernels occasionally. Once cooked sprinkle the chopped rosemary over and allow to rest for at least 10 minutes in a warm place.

The emulsion
While the lamb is cooking and resting, place all of the ingredients together in a blender or mortar and pestle. Liquidise or pound until totally fine then season.

Serving
Reheat the lamb, chickpeas and pine kernels for about 2 minutes in the oven. Dress the spinach with the pine kernel emulsion and place in the bottom of four plates or a serving dish. Carve each best end into 6, and place on top of the spinach. Scatter the chickpeas and pine kernels over and serve.

Previous page:

Glazed lamb shanks

(see page 224)

GLAZED LAMB SHANKS

SERVES 4

Planning ahead
The entire dish may be made in advance and then gently reheated.

4×300g lamb shanks, bones cleaned by your butcher
50g unsalted butter
50ml plain olive oil
8 small turnips, peeled and quartered
8 large shallots or 4 medium-small onions, peeled
4 medium carrots, peeled and halved
1 *bouquet garni* (2 sprigs of thyme, 1 bay leaf, 1 twig of rosemary)
sea salt and freshly ground black pepper
1 celery heart, trimmed and cut into 4 lengthways
8 garlic cloves, peeled

Method
Heat the butter and oil together in a large, heavy casserole on a medium heat, then caramelise the lamb shanks for 8–10 minutes. Remove the shanks and caramelise half the turnips, shallots and carrots for 5 minutes. Drain off the fat, return the shanks to the pan with the caramelised vegetables, and cover with water. Bring to the boil, skim, then add the *bouquet garni* and a pinch of salt. Simmer the lamb for 1¼ hours. Remove and discard the flavouring vegetables from the juices, and add the remaining vegetables, including the celery and garlic. Cook on for a further 45 minutes. Remove the shanks and vegetables carefully to an oven dish or tray using a slotted spoon, discarding the celery and garlic.

Preheat the oven to 200°C/400°F/Gas 6.

Skim the fat off the top of the stock, then strain. Heat two large pans and divide the stock between them. Reduce to a good texture, about 100ml per pan. Pour the stock over the top of the shanks, then place in the oven for 20 minutes, basting regularly until they have a shining glaze. Serve with the vegetables – or with buttered cabbage and French beans.

RB's note
The shanks must be cooked very slowly, at below simmering point, so that they remain moist and tender; cooked at too high a temperature, they will toughen and become stringy.

SPRING NAVARIN OF LAMB WITH FRICASSÉE OF BEANS

Nutritional note

The lamb is a good source of first-class protein, and because it is cooked slowly, it is not 'charred' and can be assimilated easily. The sugar-snap peas, runner beans, peas and broad beans are all Superfoods, and provide protein, carbohydrate, fibre and minerals. Garlic, a Superfood (see Appendix) as well, helps to enhance the immune system, and has many beneficial properties.

SERVES 4

The *navarin* is one of the highlights of French peasant cooking – honest food that follows common sense. Spring lamb, in this case the neck, served with spring vegetables.

Planning ahead
Feel free to prepare the *navarin* up to 2 days in advance. The beans may be blanched a few hours ahead of serving to be reheated with the butter and shallots later.

8 x 200g slices of neck of lamb, bone in
50ml groundnut oil
salt and freshly ground black pepper
30g unsalted butter
10g chickpea flour, toasted for 3 minutes until golden brown
100ml dry white wine, reduced by a third
4 garlic cloves, peeled and halved
1 *bouquet garni* (1 bay leaf, 2 sprigs savory, a few parsley sprigs)
2 sprigs of fresh savory, leaves picked and finely chopped

THE *FRICASSÉE* OF BEANS
200g sugar-snap peas, trimmed if necessary
200g runner beans, cut into chunks at a slant
100g podded peas
100g podded broad beans
30g butter
1 large shallot, peeled and finely chopped
3 large sprigs of fresh savory, leaves picked and finely chopped

Method
Preheat the oven to 110°C/225°F/Gas ¼.

The *navarin*
In a saucepan just large enough to hold the slices of lamb neck, heat the groundnut oil. Season the lamb well and add to the pan in a single layer. Sear and colour the lamb well for 10 minutes. Adjust the heat as necessary to ensure that it doesn't burn.

Pour off the fat and add the butter. Colour the lamb for a further 5 minutes over a medium heat making sure that the butter does not brown too much. Pour away the butter, then spoon in the toasted flour and wine. Mix well to combine. Cover with just enough water to reach the level of the lamb. Add the garlic and the *bouquet garni*. Turn up the heat and bring the mixture to the boil, stirring to make sure that there are no lumps.

Place in the preheated oven for $1^1/_2$–$1^3/_4$ hours, checking every now and then that the liquid does not come anywhere near boiling point; ideally the lamb will cook at 80°C/176°F.

Once cooked, remove the lamb from the cooking liquor and set aside. Reduce the stock over the highest possible heat, until it becomes concentrated in flavour and achieves a slightly syrupy texture, about 10 minutes.

Remove the *bouquet garni*, season the stock to taste, and place the lamb back into it. Add the savory leaves and keep warm.

The *fricassée* and serving

Prepare the peas and beans. Blanch the sugar-snap peas and runner beans in boiling salted water for 3 minutes, then refresh them in cold water. Blanch the podded peas and broad beans for 1 minute, then refresh. Drain well.

In a large frying pan melt the butter, add the chopped shallot and sweat for 2 minutes without colouring until soft. Add all the blanched vegetables and turn up the heat. Warm these through for about 2 minutes, then add the savory leaves.

Season and divide the mixture between four deep plates. Top each with 2 slices of lamb, pour the sauce over, and serve.

RB's notes

It is necessary to caramelise the lamb very well. This gives an appealing colour, but also concentrates the flavour of the lamb and contributes enormously to the flavour of the sauce.

The lamb must cook at a temperature of 80°C/176°F, very slowly so that it remains moist and succulent. Cooking it at a higher temperature will cause it to become dry and flaky. We have found that an oven temperature of 110°C/225°F/Gas $^1/_4$ is ideal.

Variations

I have chosen here a mixture of beans but, if you prefer, you could use young turnips, carrots or spring cabbage. If you have a garden, just use whatever is around at the time.

LOIN OF LAMB WITH COUSCOUS AND RED PEPPER CHUTNEY

SERVES 4

Planning ahead
The chutney will keep for a couple of days in the fridge.

4 boneless loins of lamb, approx. 150g each
salt and freshly ground black pepper
2 tbsp olive oil
150g couscous, soaked in 300ml hot water for 1 hour
10 fresh basil leaves, freshly torn

THE CHUTNEY/VINAIGRETTE
2 large red peppers, seeded and cut into strips
140ml olive oil
2 tsp liquid honey
2 tbsp fructose
3 tbsp white wine vinegar
1 red onion, peeled and finely diced
3 garlic cloves, peeled and diced
200ml *Brown Chicken Stock* (see page 36)

Method

The chutney/vinaigrette
Sear the peppers in 4 tbsp of the olive oil for 3 minutes. Add the honey, fructose, vinegar, diced red onion and garlic, cover and then allow to simmer over a medium heat for 10 minutes until the peppers soften. Remove from the heat and add the remaining olive oil and the stock. Season to taste and set aside.

The lamb and serving
Season the loin fillets and heat a pan with the olive oil. Place the lamb in the pan and cook over a medium heat for 2½ minutes each side. Remove from the heat and leave in the pan for a further 5 minutes to rest, turning it once or twice during this time.

While the lamb rests, heat through the red pepper chutney and the couscous. Remove the lamb from the pan and pour any juices from it into the chutney. Serve the lamb on top of the couscous, surrounded by, but not covered with the chutney/vinaigrette, and sprinkled with the basil.

LAMBS' KIDNEYS WITH LETTUCE AND PEAS

I have tried many ways to cook lambs' kidneys, but have never yet come up with one better than this, the most classic.

SERVES 4

10 lambs' kidneys, halved and fat removed
2 tbsp groundnut oil
salt and freshly ground black pepper
80g unsalted butter
2 shallots, peeled and finely diced
1 small bunch of fresh parsley, leaves picked and finely chopped

THE VEGETABLES

2 onions, peeled and sliced
50g unsalted butter
1 large lettuce (Reine de Glace or Butterhead), leaves picked and coarsely chopped
200g podded peas

Method

For the vegetables, sweat the sliced onion in the butter over a medium heat for 8–10 minutes. Cover just to the level of the onion with water, then add the lettuce. Cook just until the lettuce is soft then add the peas. Season well and keep warm.

Heat the groundnut oil in a frying pan, season the kidneys, then fry them over a high heat for 3 minutes until golden brown. Turn the kidneys, and lower the heat slightly. Add the butter and the chopped shallot, then fry for a further 2 minutes. Add the parsley and keep warm.

Serve the kidneys in warmed bowls on top of the onion, lettuce and pea mixture.

Variation

Mustard seeds that have been soaked overnight in white wine would make a welcome addition to the lettuce and pea mixture.

STUFFED BEEFSTEAK TOMATOES MAMAN BLANC

Nutritional note

The pork stuffing provides an excellent source of protein. The dish would attract children, giving them many Superfoods (onion, garlic, olive oil, parsley). Tomatoes are an excellent vegetable to encourage children to eat and enjoy.

SERVES 4

8 large, very ripe and firm beefsteak tomatoes
1 large onion, peeled and finely chopped
4 garlic cloves, peeled and finely chopped
3 tbsp olive oil
400g minced pork (a third fat)
1 free-range egg
1 small bunch of fresh parsley, leaves picked and chopped
80g wholemeal breadcrumbs
salt and freshly ground black pepper
1 recipe chunky *Tomato Sauce* (see page 39)

Method

Preheat the oven to 180°C/350°F/Gas 4.

Slice the tops from the tomatoes and hollow out the centres, leaving about 2cm of flesh. Chop the seeds and interior flesh to add to the sauce. Set aside.

Sweat the onion and garlic in the olive oil for 5 minutes, remove from the heat and allow to cool.

Once cooled, mix with the pork, egg, parsley and breadcrumbs, then season well with salt and pepper. Fill the tomatoes with this and place the lids back on.

Pour the tomato sauce and the chopped tomato centres into an ovenproof dish and top with the stuffed tomatoes. Bake uncovered in the preheated oven for 20 minutes, then serve immediately.

Variations

The tomato provides a vessel for just about any stuffing you like. It would be excellent with seasoned rice or flaked cod, perhaps a little ratatouille with some Parmesan, it's up to you.

CUTLET OF PORK WITH A MUSHROOM SOY JUS AND PAK-CHOI

SERVES 4

Planning ahead

The mushroom and sauce may be prepared up to 2 hours in advance and reheated. The *pak-choi* may be blanched up to 6 hours in advance.

4 cutlets of free-range pork, each weighing 200g
4 tbsp groundnut oil
salt and freshly ground black pepper
1 garlic clove, peeled and finely chopped
1 x 3cm piece of fresh root ginger, peeled and very finely chopped
20g unsalted butter
2 tbsp soy sauce

THE MUSHROOMS/SAUCE

200g shiitake mushrooms, stalks trimmed and washed
200g enoki mushrooms, stalks trimmed
1 tbsp sesame oil
2 tbsp groundnut oil
2 heads baby green *pak-choi*, each cut in 4, blanched and refreshed
150ml *Brown Chicken Stock* (see page 36)
2 tbsp thick dark soy sauce
$^1/_4$ tsp cornflour, dissolved in 20ml water

Method

Preheat the oven to 190°C/375°F/Gas 5.

The pork

Heat the groundnut oil in an ovenproof frying pan. Season the pork cutlets well and place them into the frying pan. Fry them for $1^1/_2$ minutes each side then place them into the preheated oven. After 3 minutes remove them from the oven, pour off the fat and add the garlic, ginger and butter. Place back in the oven for a further 3 minutes.

Once cooked pour off the butter, place the pan back over a high heat and add the soy sauce. Boil for 30 seconds until almost completely evaporated. Place the cutlets in a warm place to rest for at least 6 minutes.

The mushrooms/sauce

While the pork is resting, heat a deep frying pan with the sesame and groundnut oils. Add the shiitakes, and sauté for 1 minute, then add the enoki mushrooms, the *pak-choi* and the stock. Boil rapidly for 1 minute then add the soy sauce. Bring to the boil, add the dissolved cornflour, and bring back to the boil, stirring constantly. Set aside and keep warm.

Serving

Spoon the mushrooms, *pak-choi* and sauce into four deep plates and top with the pork cutlets.

Variation

This recipe would be equally good using chicken or duck in place of the pork. The mushrooms may be varied to suit your preferences and their availability.

PORK CUTLETS WITH LENTILS

SERVES 4

4 cutlets of free-range pork, each weighing approx. 200g
3 tbsp groundnut oil
salt and freshly ground black pepper

THE LENTILS

150g lentils
1 large onion, peeled and finely diced
2 tbsp groundnut oil
1 large sprig of fresh thyme
2 bay leaves
grated zest and juice of 2 unsprayed lemons

THE MUSTARD BUTTER

60g unsalted butter
1 large bunch of fresh parsley, leaves picked and finely chopped
30g grain mustard

Method

The lentils

In a large saucepan cover the lentils with cold water and bring them to the boil. Strain into a colander and rinse them off under cold water. Sweat the chopped onion in the groundnut oil for 2 minutes, then add the lentils and enough water just to cover them. Add the thyme, bay leaves and lemon zest and bring to the boil. Cook at just below simmering point for 25 minutes or until soft (the cooking time will depend on the age of the lentils). Once cooked, remove from the heat, season with salt, black pepper and lemon juice, then set aside.

The mustard butter

Mix all the ingredients together, roll into a sausage shape in a piece of clingfilm, and reserve in the fridge.

The pork and serving

Preheat the grill to its highest setting. Heat the groundnut oil in a large frying pan, season the pork cutlets well then fry them for 4 minutes on each side over a medium heat. Allow to rest for a further 4 minutes. Heat the lentils and slice the mustard butter into 4 pieces. Place a piece of the mustard butter on top of each cutlet and grill them until the butter is half melted. Serve the cutlets on top of the lentils.

DAUBE OF BEEF WITH ORANGE

SERVES 4

Planning ahead
The entire dish may be made up to 2 days in advance and reheated gently for serving.

1kg chuck beef, cut into 20 x 50g pieces
50ml groundnut oil
salt and freshly ground black pepper
30g butter
24 baby onions, peeled
8 garlic cloves, peeled and halved
2 tbsp cornflour
1 bottle full-bodied red wine, reduced by half
500ml *Brown Chicken Stock* (see page 36)
100g stoned black olives
1 bouquet garni (2 bay leaves and 1 large sprig of thyme)
zest of 1 unsprayed orange, removed with a vegetable peeler

Method
Preheat the oven to 110°C/225°F/Gas ¼.

Heat the groundnut oil in a large ovenproof pan. Season the beef well then sear and colour it for 5 minutes. Reduce the heat and add the butter, then caramelise for a further 10 minutes. Add the baby onions and garlic, and sweat for 1 minute.

Remove the excess fat from the pan, then add the cornflour, stirring well to make absolutely sure that no lumps form. Add the reduced red wine gradually, along with the chicken stock (or water), and add the *bouquet garni* and orange zest. Bring to the boil and skim, then place into the preheated oven and braise for 2 hours. Remove from the oven, add the olives, season to taste, and serve.

RB's notes
Braising at 110°C/225°F/Gas ¼ will cook the beef at 80°C/176°F. This results in a dish which is moist, tender and full of flavour. Too high a temperature will cause the meat to be tough and dry.

PAN-FRIED RIBEYE STEAKS WITH MUSTARD PEPPER CRUST

SERVES 4

Planning ahead

The crust may be made a day or so in advance.

4 ribeye steaks, each weighing 250g
4 tbsp grain mustard
1 tbsp white peppercorns, crushed
20g fresh grated horseradish, or 40g bottled
6 large sprigs of fresh flat-leaf parsley, leaves picked, washed and sliced
40g butter, melted
4 tbsp groundnut oil
salt and freshly ground black pepper
30g butter
2 large shallots, peeled and finely diced
200g green beans, blanched for 3 minutes

Method

Preheat the grill to its hottest setting.

Mix together the grain mustard, crushed peppercorns, horseradish, flat-leaf parsley and melted butter.

Heat a large pan with the groundnut oil. Season the ribeyes and fry for about 3½ minutes on each side for medium rare, longer if you like them more well done. Transfer the steaks to a warmed plate to rest.

Pour off the fat in the pan and add the butter. Spoon in the chopped shallot and sweat for 2 minutes, then add the beans and sauté for a further couple of minutes until they are warmed through.

Spread the mustard crust over the ribeyes, place under the grill for a minute, and serve with the beans.

VEAL ESCALOPE WITH SPINACH, PEAS AND MUSTARD CREAM

SERVES 4

Planning ahead
The sauce may be made in advance and reheated.

4 escalopes of veal, weighing 175g each
5 tbsp olive oil
salt and freshly ground black pepper
300g spinach, leaves picked and washed
200g podded peas

THE MUSTARD CREAM
150ml *White Chicken Stock* (see page 35)
100ml whipping cream
1½ tbsp Dijon mustard

Method
First make the mustard cream. Bring the stock to the boil then add the cream and whisk in the Dijon mustard. Season and set aside.

Heat a large pan with 3 tbsp of the olive oil, season the veal escalopes and fry them for 2 minutes on each side. Remove them from the pan to a warmed plate and allow to rest.

Heat the pan again and add the remaining olive oil and the spinach. Sauté for a minute or two until the spinach begins to wilt, then add the peas and heat through. Season well. Serve the veal on top of the vegetables, covered with the mustard cream.

Variation
This idea would be equally good with turkey escalopes or chicken breasts.

CALF'S LIVER WITH RED ONION MARMALADE

Nutritional note

Liver is an excellent source of B vitamins as well as protein. The potato adds carbohydrate, as does the onion marmalade. Because onions contain sugars, these can be caramelised, and will add some sweetness to the dish.

SERVES 4

4 x 150g slices of calf's liver
3 tbsp groundnut oil
salt and freshly ground black pepper
2 tbsp sherry vinegar or white wine vinegar

THE RED ONION MARMALADE
4 large red onions, peeled and finely sliced
2 tbsp groundnut oil
2 tbsp sherry vinegar or white wine vinegar

THE CRUSHED POTATOES
4 medium floury potatoes
80ml olive oil

Method

The red onion marmalade
Sweat the sliced red onions for 15 minutes in the groundnut oil until totally soft. Raise the heat and evaporate all of the liquid, then add the sherry vinegar and allow to caramelise slightly. Season to taste and set aside.

The crushed potatoes
Preheat the oven to 200°C/400°F/Gas 6. Bake the potatoes in foil for an hour or so until soft. Peel them while still hot and place the flesh into a bowl. Add the olive oil and mash together with a fork. Don't try to get it too fine, this is intended to be a rough-textured purée. Season and keep warm.

The liver
Heat a frying pan with the groundnut oil, season the liver and fry over a brisk heat for about $1^{1}/_{2}$ minutes each side. Add the sherry vinegar and reduce to 1 tbsp.

Serving
Heat the red onion marmalade and spread it across the bottom of four warmed plates. Divide the crushed potato between the centres of these plates and top with the slices of calf's liver. Place the liver pan back on the heat and stir in a little water to make a *jus*. Pour this over the top of the liver and serve.

POUSSIN WITH HERBS AND BRAISED AUBERGINE

SERVES 4

Planning ahead
The aubergine, cooked as it is in olive oil, keeps extremely well and can be made 2 days in advance.

4 free-range *poussins*, each weighing 350g, cut in half down the
    backbone (ask your butcher to do this for you)
grated zest of 1 unsprayed lemon
50ml extra virgin olive oil
1 bunch of fresh parsley, leaves picked and chopped
10 fresh oregano leaves, chopped
1 red chilli, seeded and finely chopped

THE AUBERGINE *CONFIT*
2 medium aubergines, approx. 800g in total, peeled
100ml olive oil
1 red chilli, seeded and finely chopped
juice of 1 unsprayed lemon

Method

The aubergine *confit*
Cut the aubergines in half, into thick slices, then into French-fry-sized strips. Place in a pan with the olive oil, chilli and lemon juice, then braise over a medium heat for 10 minutes. Reserve until needed.

The *poussins*
Preheat the grill to its highest setting.
   Mix the lemon zest, olive oil, parsley, oregano and chilli together and force two-thirds of it underneath the skin of the *poussins*. Place them skin side up on a roasting tray and grill them for 12 minutes, lowering the shelf if the skin starts to get too dark. Once cooked allow to rest for a couple of minutes.

Serving
Heat up the aubergine *confit*, and spoon into the centres of four large plates or a serving dish. Top with the *poussin* halves, and pour any juices that remain in the bottom of the tray over. Sprinkle with the rest of the herb, chilli and lemon mixture, and serve.

CHICKEN WITH FLAGEOLET BEANS

SERVES 4

1 large free-range roasting chicken, cut into 8 pieces (ask your butcher to
    do this for you)
4 tbsp groundnut oil
salt and freshly ground black pepper

THE BEANS

200g flageolet beans, soaked for 12 hours
40g unsalted butter
1 large onion, peeled and finely sliced
1 small head of Swiss chard, stalks chopped, leaves roughly shredded
1 heaped tbsp grain mustard (or more depending on taste)

Method

The beans

Drain the water from the flageolet beans and rinse them well. Place them in a
large saucepan with plenty of fresh water, bring them to the boil, then strain
into a colander and rinse well.

In another saucepan, melt the butter and add the sliced onion, Swiss chard
stalks and the strained beans. Sweat this together over a low heat for about 5
minutes. Cover with water and simmer for $1\frac{1}{2}$ hours or until soft. Top up the
water as necessary during the cooking time so that the beans are constantly
only just submerged.

Once cooked, remove about a quarter of the bean mixture, then liquidise
this in a food processor until you have a fine purée. Add this back to the rest of
the beans. Stir in the grain mustard and season to taste.

The chicken and serving

Preheat the oven to 180°C/350°F/Gas 4.

Heat the groundnut oil in an ovenproof dish, season the chicken pieces well
then fry them skin side down over a medium high heat for about 5 minutes
until they are well browned. Remove the chicken from the dish then pour off
the fat. Add the bean mixture to the dish and stir in the shredded chard leaves.
Top this with the pieces of chicken, cover with a piece of tin foil, then bake in
the preheated oven for 30 minutes. Serve immediately.

BREAST OF FREE-RANGE CHICKEN IN A VEGETABLE NAGE

SERVES 4

Planning ahead
The vegetable *nage* may be made 3 days in advance and kept refrigerated.

4 breasts of free-range chicken, each weighing 180g
2 garlic cloves, peeled and finely chopped
4 sprigs of fresh marjoram, leaves picked and finely chopped
salt and freshly ground black pepper
2 tbsp groundnut oil
1 recipe *Vegetable Nage* (see page 37)

THE GARNISH
20 calamata olives, stoned and cut in half
12 cherry tomatoes, cut in half
1 bunch of rocket, finely chopped
40ml olive oil

Method

The chicken
Preheat the oven to 180°C/350°F/Gas 4.

Loosen the skin from the chicken breasts, and slip a little of the garlic and marjoram in between the flesh and skin of each. Season them well.

In an ovenproof pan, heat the groundnut oil and place the chicken breasts in, skin side down. Fry them over a gentle heat for 4 minutes then place them in the preheated oven for 8 minutes. Check to make sure they are totally cooked, and keep warm.

Finishing and serving
Heat the vegetable *nage* through. Place the chicken breasts into the vegetable *nage*, add the olives, tomatoes and rocket and bring to the boil. Season with salt if necessary and freshly ground black pepper. Spoon the vegetables and *nage* into four bowls, place the chicken on top, and drizzle the olive oil over. Serve.

Variation
This dish would work well with guinea fowl instead of chicken.

ROASTED QUAIL WITH POLENTA AND WILD MUSHROOMS

SERVES 4

8 free-range quails, well cleaned
30g dried ceps, soaked in 200ml water
4 tbsp groundnut oil
salt and freshly ground black pepper
200g mixed wild mushrooms, washed and cut in half
2 tbsp unsalted butter
4 sprigs of fresh savory or thyme, leaves picked and chopped

THE POLENTA
150g polenta
750ml water
50g Parmesan, grated
50g mascarpone cheese

Method

The polenta
Bring the water to the boil with a little salt, and add the polenta in a steady stream, stirring constantly. Allow to cook, stirring frequently, for about 45 minutes. Stir in the Parmesan and mascarpone, season to taste, and keep warm.

The quails and sauce
Preheat the oven to 200°C/400°F/Gas 6.

Strain the ceps through a fine sieve, being careful to keep all of the soaking liquor. Rinse them under cold water and chop them coarsely. Set aside.

Heat the oil in an ovenproof frying pan then season and sear the quails for 2–3 minutes on each side until they are well browned. Add the wild mushrooms and ceps to the pan, then cook for a further couple of minutes.

Add the juice from the ceps, the butter and savory or thyme to the pan, then place in the oven and cook for 4 minutes, turning the quails once during this time. Once cooked, allow to rest for about 5 minutes.

Serving
Serve the quails on top of the polenta, well covered with the sauce and, if you feel like it, a drizzle of a peppery Tuscan olive oil.

ASIAN POT-AU-FEU

SERVES 4

4 large breasts of free-range chicken
salt and freshly ground black pepper
2 large carrots, peeled and sliced
2 large turnips, peeled and cut into segments
1 x 6cm piece of fresh root ginger, finely chopped
4 garlic cloves, peeled and chopped
100ml soy sauce
1 large head of broccoli, cut into florets
100g soba noodles, blanched for 5 minutes and refreshed

Method

In a large pan of boiling salted water, blanch the carrots and turnips for 5 minutes. Drain and place in a saucepan large enough to hold everything. Top with the seasoned chicken breasts. Tie the ginger and garlic together in a small muslin bag so that they are easy to remove once the dish is cooked. Add to the pan with the soy sauce, then cover with water and cook at just below simmering point for 15 minutes.

Add the broccoli and cook for a further 5 minutes. Check that the chicken breasts are cooked, then add the blanched soba noodles and heat them through.

Serve the chicken, noodles and vegetables in large bowls with the broth.

Variations

Any poultry would be fine for this dish, and the vegetables can also be changed to suit your taste: a member of the Chinese cabbage family such as *pak-choi* would make a welcome addition.

If you don't like it, you can remove the skin of the chicken, but do so after the chicken is cooked or the flesh will become very dry.

This recipe gives a very light fresh tasting broth; if you prefer a more concentrated flavour, you could use *White Chicken Stock* (see page 35) instead of water.

SOY-MARINATED CHICKEN BREASTS WITH CUCUMBER VINAIGRETTE

SERVES 4

Planning ahead
The chicken may be marinated a day or so in advance, in the refrigerator.

4 boneless and skinless breasts of free-range chicken
4 tbsp thick dark soy sauce
3 tsp liquid honey
salt and cayenne pepper
2 tbsp sesame seeds
2 tbsp groundnut oil
500g young spinach, leaves picked and washed

THE VINAIGRETTE
2 tbsp rice (or white wine) vinegar
2 tbsp water
80ml groundnut oil
4 shallots, peeled and thinly sliced
1 English cucumber, seeded and cut into 2cm dice
1 small bunch of fresh coriander, leaves picked and sliced

Method
Stir the soy and honey together with 2 good pinches of cayenne pepper. Add the chicken breasts to this and turn well so that they are completely coated. Allow to marinate for at least 1 hour.

Meanwhile, make the vinaigrette. Mix the vinegar together with the water and a little salt, then whisk in the groundnut oil. Add the vegetables and coriander, then set aside.

Preheat the oven to 180°C/350°F/Gas 4.

To cook the chicken, simply place the breasts into an ovenproof dish with the marinade and bake in the preheated oven for 10 minutes. Sprinkle the sesame seeds over the top and cook for a further 5 minutes. Remove from the oven and allow to rest in a warm place.

In a very hot pan, heat the groundnut oil and stir-fry the spinach for about 1 minute until softened. Place this into four warmed plates. Top with the chicken and any of the marinade that remains in the pan, spoon around the vinaigrette and serve.

ROASTED GUINEA FOWL WITH CONFIT OF BEETROOT

SERVES 4

Planning ahead

The beetroot may be boiled, peeled and cut the day before.

1 free-range guinea fowl, weighing approx. 1.2kg, cleaned and trussed
4 large beetroot, approx. 800g in all, washed but not peeled
salt and freshly ground black pepper
4 tbsp groundnut oil
2 tbsp red wine vinegar
5 sprigs of fresh thyme
200ml water
100ml olive oil

Method

The beetroot

Preheat the oven to 200°C/400°F/Gas 6.

Cook the beetroot in plenty of salted water until soft; this will generally take about an hour, but depends on the age of your beetroot. Once cooked, put on a pair of gloves and peel them. Slice the beetroot or cut them into cubes, whichever you prefer, then set aside.

The guinea fowl

Heat the groundnut oil in a large pan then sear and colour the guinea fowl for 4 minutes on each side. Add the beetroot, vinegar and thyme to the pan and place into the preheated oven to roast for a further 15 minutes on each side.

Once cooked remove from the oven, and lift the guinea fowl up so that the juices drain into the pan with the beetroot. Put the guinea fowl in a warm place to rest.

Place the pan with the beetroot over a high heat, add the water and bring to the boil. Add the olive oil, and remove from the heat. Season to taste and keep warm.

Serving

Carve the guinea fowl (see page 259). Roll the guinea fowl in the pan juices to give it a lovely glaze, and serve on top of the beetroot and sauce.

CHICKEN BREAST WITH COCONUT AND CARDAMOM

Nutritional note

The chicken breasts are good protein without significant amounts of saturated fat. The coconut milk provides essential oil. Coriander, cardamom, garlic, onion and chilli are all Superfoods (see Appendix). The brown basmati rice provides B vitamins as well as good carbohydrate.

SERVES 4

Planning ahead

The chicken needs to be marinated, in the refrigerator, for 6 to 24 hours. The spring onion mixture can be made 2–3 hours before serving.

4 breasts of free-range chicken, about 200g each, skinned
1 tsp coriander seeds, finely crushed
1 tsp cardamom pods, finely crushed
2 garlic cloves, peeled and crushed
350ml unsweetened coconut milk
300g brown basmati rice
1 bunch of spring onions, finely cut at a slant
1 bunch of fresh coriander, leaves picked and sliced
1 small red chilli, seeded and finely chopped
6 tbsp groundnut oil
grated zest and juice of 1 unsprayed lemon
salt and freshly ground black pepper

Method

Mix together the crushed coriander seeds, cardamom and garlic and rub into the breasts of chicken. Place in a container, add the coconut milk, then mix well and allow to marinate for at least 6 hours.

Preheat the oven to 190°C/375°F/Gas 5.

Cook the brown basmati rice for 35–40 minutes in plenty of boiling water. Drain well and keep warm.

While the rice is cooking, mix together the spring onions, fresh coriander, chilli, 2 tbsp of the groundnut oil, the lemon juice and zest. Season well and set aside.

Remove the chicken from its marinade, scrape off the spices, and pat dry. Heat a large frying pan with the remaining groundnut oil, season the chicken breasts and fry them for 2 minutes on each side. Transfer them to a warmed plate.

Drain any fat remaining in the pan, and add the strained coconut marinade. Place the chicken breasts back into it, then put the pan into the preheated oven for 10–15 minutes. Remove the chicken from the pan and if the sauce has separated slightly, add a little water and whisk it back together. Season to taste.

Serve the chicken and sauce on top of the rice, and cover with the spring onion mixture.

POUSSIN WITH A VEGETABLE BROTH

Nutritional note

The *poussin* provides the protein here, the root vegetables carbohydrate, and the leeks and beans add carbohydrate, fibre, minerals and vitamins. A good contrasting flavour is that of the horseradish, which is a stimulant of salivary and other digestive juices.

SERVES 4

This is a dish that is ideal for someone living alone; the baby chickens or *poussins* provide a perfect portion, and are available almost anywhere.

4 very fresh, free-range *poussins*
2 large leeks, well washed and thinly sliced
2 large carrots, peeled, halved and thinly sliced
2 turnips, peeled and cut into wedges
500ml *White Chicken Stock* (see page 35)
200g runner beans, cut into 2cm slices, blanched for 2 minutes and refreshed
2 tbsp grated fresh horseradish
1 large bunch of fresh chervil, leaves picked
sea salt and freshly ground black pepper

Method

The *poussins* and vegetables

Place the leek, carrot and turnip in the bottom of a pan that is just large enough to hold all of the vegetables and the *poussins*. Top with the *poussins* and pour the stock over; if it does not completely cover them, just add a little water so that they are completely submerged. Bring all of this to the boil and cook at just below simmering point for 20–25 minutes until you can lift the *poussins* and the liquid that comes out is totally clear.

While the *poussins* are cooking, skim the liquid frequently to remove any impurities that rise; this will give you a wonderfully clear broth.

Once cooked add the runner beans, horseradish and chervil to the broth, and season to taste.

Serving

It is totally up to you. This dish can be served as a traditional *pot-au-feu* in a big dish or tureen at the table, with salt and freshly ground pepper on the side for every one to help themselves, perhaps starting with the broth, then going on to the vegetables and finishing with the poussins. Alternatively, it makes quite an elegant presentation all together in large, deep soup plates.

Variation

If you don't want to use *poussins* you could make the same dish using boiling fowl. Just add about 20 minutes' cooking time, and cut the vegetables into bigger pieces.

WOOD PIGEON WITH PAN-FRIED RADICCHIO

This dish is made using only the breasts of the pigeon as the legs have a tendency to be very tough. The breasts must be cooked at most to medium rare as, if they are cooked more, they become dry very quickly.

SERVES 4

Planning ahead
The shallot-anchovy mixture can easily be prepared a few hours in advance. You may also blanch, refresh and dry the radicchio at the same time.

8 breasts of wood pigeon (ask your butcher to remove them for you and, if you like, keep the carcass and legs to make a stock or soup)
6 small heads of radicchio, blanched for 5 minutes, refreshed then squeezed dry
4 tbsp olive oil
salt and freshly ground black pepper
4 large sprigs each of fresh thyme and rosemary, leaves picked and finely chopped
4 large shallots, peeled and finely chopped
8 anchovy fillets, rinsed and finely chopped
6 tbsp extra virgin olive oil

Method
Heat a frying pan or griddle with the olive oil. Season the pigeon breasts well and fry them, skin side down, over a high heat for 2 minutes. Add the radicchio and fry together for a further 3 minutes.

While these are cooking, mix together the thyme, rosemary, shallots, anchovies and extra virgin olive oil. Add a little black pepper and set aside.

Turn the pigeon on to the flesh side and remove from the heat. Allow to rest for 2 minutes.

Spread the herb, shallot and anchovy mixture across the top of the breasts, and serve these on top of the radicchio. If you like, sprinkle with a little more olive oil and some red wine vinegar.

RB's note
The addition of anchovy may seem a little strange but it is used as a seasoning, and I assure you goes very well.

WHOLEMEAL RAVIOLI IN A CHICKEN BROTH WITH ROAST GARLIC

SERVES 4

THE PASTA DOUGH
250g wholemeal flour
1 whole free-range egg plus 3 egg yolks
1 tbsp olive oil

THE FILLING
2 large shallots, peeled and finely chopped
3 tbsp olive oil
100g rocket, roughly chopped
200g watercress, roughly chopped
200g ricotta cheese
salt and freshly ground black pepper

THE BROTH
2 tbsp olive oil
12 garlic cloves, peeled and blanched for 5 minutes
800ml *White Chicken Stock* (see page 35)
100g rocket

Method

The ravioli
To make the pasta, mix the flour, eggs and olive oil together in a food processor until they form a ball. Add a little water if necessary to bind. Wrap in clingfilm and allow to rest for half an hour.

For the filling, sweat the shallot in the olive oil for about 2 minutes, then add the chopped rocket and watercress and sauté briskly for about 30 seconds. Remove from the heat, mix in the ricotta and season well. Set aside.

Shape the pasta into two rectangles and roll them out to number 5 on your machine (or thinly, if rolling by hand). Lightly flour your work surface with wholemeal flour and lay the sheets across it.

Cut out 20 x 10cm circles and place a small spoonful of the rocket mixture in the centre of each, making sure to leave enough space at the sides so that you are able to close them into half-moon shapes and seal the edges. This is a good time if possible to get a hand from someone as the pasta will dry fairly quickly. Blanch them in plenty of boiling salted water then transfer to iced water to refresh.

Once cooled remove from the water and reserve until needed.

The broth and serving
Heat the olive oil in a deep pan and add the blanched garlic. Sauté until well browned then add the chicken stock. Bring to the boil, skim and then simmer for about 5 minutes. Add the ravioli to heat through, then the rocket leaves, just until they are softened. Spoon into bowls and serve.

Variations
If you cannot find any rocket, you could substitute a mixture of watercress and spinach, or just watercress. If you have any turnips in the garden, their leaves may be used.

DUCK BREASTS WITH BROCCOLI AND CAULIFLOWER

SERVES 4

4 duck breasts, each approx. 200g, with skin lightly criss-cross scored
3 tbsp groundnut oil
1 small head of broccoli, cut into florets and blanched
1 small cauliflower, cut into florets and blanched
2 heads of *choi-sum*, roughly chopped
4 tbsp sesame seeds
1 x 6cm piece of fresh root ginger, peeled and finely chopped
3 tbsp soy sauce

Method
Preheat the oven to 200°C/400°F/Gas 6.

Place the duck breasts skin side down into a warm ovenproof frying pan. Dry-fry over a medium heat for about 5–6 minutes until the skin is a golden brown colour and most of the fat has been rendered. Pour off the fat then place the breasts in the oven for 6 minutes. Once cooked, remove from the oven and allow to rest in a warm place.

Meanwhile, heat a wok or large frying pan with the groundnut oil and add the broccoli, cauliflower, *choi-sum* and sesame seeds. Stir-fry for 2–3 minutes then add the ginger, soy sauce and a little water. Fry for a further minute then spoon on to four warmed plates and top with the duck breasts. Serve.

GLAZED BREASTS OF MALLARD WITH BUTTERNUT SQUASH

Ideally, if your butcher is agreeable, ask for 2 crowns of wild duck so that you can cook the breast on the bone. This gives you a greater flavour, keeps the flesh moister and also allows you to cook the meat well in advance.

Nutritional note

Wild duck are not so fatty as domesticated ducks, therefore provide less saturated fat. Honey is glycaemic to an extent, but the quantity used here is minimal. Butternut squash contains beta-carotene as well as fibre. The pine kernels add essential fats, and cumin is a Superfood (see Appendix).

SERVES 4

4 breasts of wild duck
2 tsp liquid honey
1½ tbsp cumin seeds
grated zest and juice of 1 unsprayed lime
2 tbsp groundnut oil
300ml *Brown Chicken Stock* (see page 36)
2 tbsp thick dark soy sauce

THE SQUASH

1 butternut squash, approx. 800g–1kg, peeled, cut into 3cm cubes or
   triangles and blanched for 5 minutes
4 heaped tbsp pine kernels
1 tbsp groundnut oil
juice and grated zest of 1 unsprayed lime

TO SERVE

grated zest of 1 unsprayed lime

Method

Preheat the oven to 180°C/350°F/Gas 4.

Mix the honey with the cumin seeds, lime juice and zest. Heat a pan with the groundnut oil and colour the duck crowns for 3 minutes on each breast. Remove the skin and rub the flesh with the honey, cumin and lime mixture. Place in the oven for 3 minutes. Remove and baste the breasts with the honey mixture from the pan. Transfer to a rack and allow to rest for at least 5 minutes.

Pour the chicken stock and soy sauce into the duck pan and bring to the boil, stirring. Keep warm.

Sauté the pine kernels in the groundnut oil for a couple of minutes until they begin to colour, then add the blanched squash cubes and sauté for a further 2–3 minutes until totally heated through. Stir in the lime zest and juice.

Divide the squash between four plates. Carve the duck breasts from the bone, place them on top of the squash, spoon over the sauce, sprinkle with the lime zest and serve.

GRILLED QUAIL WITH CHICKPEAS AND FENNEL

Nutritional note

Quails contain good protein, without too much saturated fat. Fennel, both bulb and herb, has a number of special properties, and prepared in this way, will intensely complement the flavour of the chickpeas. The chickpeas are a good source of fibre, vegetable protein and carbohydrate.

SERVES 4

Planning ahead

The chickpeas may be cooked and mixed with their accompaniments well ahead of time.

4 free-range quails, cleaned and cut in half (ask your butcher to do this)
4 tbsp olive oil
rock salt and freshly ground black pepper
1 small bunch of fresh fennel leaf, finely chopped

THE CHICKPEAS

300g chickpeas, freshly cooked (see page 43)
150ml extra virgin olive oil
juice of 1 unsprayed lemon
1 large onion, peeled and finely chopped
1 large fennel bulb, finely sliced

Method

Once the chickpeas are cooked, strain them from their liquid and mix them with the virgin olive oil, the lemon juice, the onion and the fennel. Set aside.

Preheat your grill to its highest setting and place the halved quails skin side up on to a tray. Brush with olive oil, and sprinkle with salt and coarsely ground black pepper. Place the quails under the grill and cook for 8 minutes, lowering the shelf if the skins start to colour too much. Turn off the grill and allow the quails to rest while you reheat the chickpeas.

Once hot, spoon the chickpeas into four plates or a serving dish, and top with the grilled quails. Sprinkle with the chopped fennel leaf, and serve.

GUINEA FOWL WITH BUTTER BEANS AND RADICCHIO

SERVES 4

1 free-range guinea fowl, weighing approx. 1.2kg
2 tbsp groundnut oil
salt and freshly ground black pepper

THE BEANS
300g butter beans, freshly cooked (see page 43) with 6 garlic cloves,
    peeled and cut in half, or tinned and drained beans
100ml extra virgin olive oil
3 heads of radicchio, leaves picked, washed and sliced
1 large bunch of fresh parsley, leaves picked and coarsely chopped

Method
Preheat the oven to 200°C/400°F/Gas 6.

The beans
When the beans are cooked, remove 3–4 spoonfuls and purée them. Add the purée back to the remainder. Add the olive oil, salt and plenty of black pepper, stir well to combine, then set aside.

The guinea fowl
Heat the groundnut oil in a large ovenproof pan, season the guinea fowl then sear for 4 minutes on each side. Transfer to the oven and roast for a further 15 minutes on each side. Once cooked, remove from the oven and allow to rest for about 10 minutes with the breast facing downwards. During this time, add the radicchio and parsley to the beans, and heat them through.

Serving
When you are carving a guinea fowl or chicken for four people you have two options. The easiest is if you have two people that like leg meat and two people that like breast meat. The other way is to cut each leg and breast in half and serve each person a piece of each. So whichever you decide, roll the guinea fowl in the pan juices to give it a lovely glaze, and serve on top of the beans.

RB's note
The guinea fowl must be free-range and hung for 8–10 days. This ensures the flavour and texture are at their best. Cook two guinea fowl if the birds are quite small.

LOIN OF VENISON WITH BUTTERNUT PURÉE AND RED WINE PEAR CHUTNEY

SERVES 4

1 x 800g fillet of venison, well matured
2 tbsp groundnut oil
salt and freshly ground black pepper
15g butter

THE PEAR CHUTNEY
2 large Comice pears, cored and cut into 2–3cm cubes
300ml red wine
3 tbsp fructose
1 tbsp cracked black pepper

THE BUTTERNUT PURÉE
1 butternut squash, about 450g, peeled, seeded and cut into 4cm pieces
100ml milk
4 tbsp hazelnut oil

Method

The pear chutney
Reduce the red wine with the fructose and black pepper by two-thirds, then add the pear cubes and simmer for 5 minutes. Set aside.

The butternut purée
Boil the butternut squash for 8–10 minutes in plenty of boiling salted water. Strain and press well to remove any excess liquid. Boil the milk and add this to the squash in the bowl of your food processor. Blend until smooth, then add the hazelnut oil and season to taste. Set aside.

The venison and serving
Preheat the oven to 200°C/400°F/Gas 6. Heat the oil in an ovenproof pan, season the venison then brown on all sides for 2 minutes. Pour off the oil, add the butter, and let the venison colour gently for a further 2 minutes. Place into the oven for a further 5 minutes then set aside in a warm place to rest.

During this time make sure the purée and chutney are hot. Remove the venison from the pan and add about 50ml water to the pan. Bring this to the boil, stirring, and season. Slice the venison into four and serve on top of the purée and chutney with the *jus* around.

CONFIT OF DUCK WITH SPINACH AND TOMATO CONFIT

SERVES 4

Planning ahead

The duck *confit* may be made as long as you like in advance.

8 duck legs
50g sea salt
1 tbsp black peppercorns, crushed
1 large sprig of fresh thyme
1 bay leaf
1 garlic clove, peeled and crushed
1 litre duck fat (if unavailable use groundnut oil)
2 fennel bulbs, cut into quarters lengthways
400g spinach, leaves picked and washed
12 black olives, halved and stoned
20 *Tomato Confit* tomatoes (see page 38)

Method

Mix the duck legs with the salt, peppercorns, thyme, bay leaf and garlic. Rub well into the duck and leave to marinate for 24 hours in a cool place.

Wipe all the spices off the duck legs, and put them into a saucepan with the duck fat and quartered fennel. Cook at just below simmering point for 1½ hours until the meat almost falls away from the bone.

Lift the duck legs and fennel from the fat with the aid of a slotted spoon. Drain the fennel on kitchen paper. Place the legs into a frying pan, skin side down. Over a medium heat fry the legs, skin side only, for 6–8 minutes until most of the fat is rendered out and the skin is crisp and brown. Remove from the pan and keep warm.

Pour off any excess fat and add the fennel, spinach, olives and tomatoes to the pan. Cook for a minute or so just until the spinach has wilted. You won't need to add any salt, so just spoon the spinach mixture into the bottom of four plates, and top with the crisp duck legs.

RABBIT WITH SPRING VEGETABLES

This dish is made using farmed rabbit, a delightful meat which is now becoming easier to find. Most quality butchers will be able, with just a little notice, to find it for you. If not, replace with chicken or guinea fowl.

Nutritional note

Making a stock with the rabbit bones is excellent, as many bones contain minerals which will leach out into the stock. The carrots and snowpeas provide excellent vegetable carbohydrate to complement the protein of the rabbit.

SERVES 4

4 fillets of farmed rabbit from the saddle (keep the bones)
4 tbsp thick soy sauce
2 medium carrots, peeled and cut into slices at a slant
salt and freshly ground black pepper
200g snowpeas, topped and tailed
8 spring onions, trimmed and halved
2 tbsp groundnut oil
1 tbsp coriander seeds

THE STOCK/VINAIGRETTE

the bones from the rabbit
50ml groundnut oil
100ml dry white wine
1 tbsp coriander seeds, lightly crushed

Method

The rabbit and vegetables

Coat the rabbit fillets with the soy sauce and leave to marinate for 2 hours.

Blanch the carrots in boiling salted water for 3 minutes. Drain and refresh. Blanch the snowpeas and spring onion for 1 minute, then drain and refresh.

The stock/vinaigrette

Heat a saucepan with 1 tbsp of the groundnut oil and add the chopped rabbit bones. Fry for about 15 minutes until golden brown. Drain off any fat and add the white wine. Reduce by half then just cover with water. Bring to the boil, skim, then allow to simmer for 20 minutes. Strain the stock, then reduce to a glaze. Add the soy marinade from the rabbit fillets, the remaining oil and the coriander seeds, then season to taste and set aside.

Cooking and serving

Preheat the oven to 200°C/400°F/Gas 6. Heat a pan with the groundnut oil, add the rabbit fillets and fry for 1 minute on each side. Place in the oven for 2 further minutes then remove and place on a warmed plate to rest. Sauté the vegetables in the same pan until warm, and add the coriander seeds. Season then serve topped with the rabbit fillets and surrounded with the vinaigrette.

BRAISED RABBIT LEGS WITH POTATOES AND PEPPERS

Don't be put off by the cooking time, this dish is actually very easy and quick to prepare. Due to the long slow cooking, the rabbit ends up moist and full of the flavours of the aromatics and vegetables cooked with it.

SERVES 4

Planning ahead

The entire dish may be made in advance and reheated.

    4 large rabbit legs
    4 tbsp olive oil
    4 tbsp polenta (optional)
    salt and freshly ground black pepper
    150ml white wine
    8 whole garlic cloves, blanched for 2 minutes and peeled
    1 pinch of dried chilli
    2 large red peppers, seeded and cut into thick strips
    400ml *White Chicken Stock* (see page 35)
    2 large new potatoes, each cut into 6
    2 sprigs of fresh rosemary, leaves picked and chopped

Method

Heat a pan large enough to hold the rabbit legs in a single layer and add the olive oil. Dust the rabbit legs with the polenta, if using, and season them well. Sear them in the olive oil for 3 minutes on each side. Add the white wine and reduce by half. Toss in the garlic, chilli and peppers, then pour the chicken stock over and bring to the boil. Skim then cook at below simmering point for half an hour.

Add the potatoes and rosemary and cook for a further hour until the meat almost falls off the bone. Season to taste and serve.

Variation

This dish may be made with free-range chicken or guinea fowl legs.

DESSERTS

This chapter was to be the biggest challenge, but actually replacing sugar with small amounts of fructose, honey and maple syrup proved to be no problem at all.

Fruits in season remain for me the basis of the most special desserts; when picked ripe, very little needs to be done to enhance them. I have also been inspired to do something like the fruit soup of blood orange and rhubarb, and to roast and grill other fruits to intensify their natural sweetness. The *pots à la crème* and *oeufs à la neige* were easily adapted to the use of fructose and these, along with the others, remain a treat to be shared and, most of all, to be enjoyed without regret.

RB

Fructose, fruit sugar, is available as a powder, a carbohydrate sweetener, which is four times sweeter than sucrose. It is not glycaemic as it is slowly broken down in the liver, and does not elevate blood sugar instantly as do some other sugars. Where concentrated sugars have been used, unrefined products have been deliberately chosen which, although containing sucrose (maple syrup 63 per cent, honey 31 per cent), also contain some of the vitamins and minerals necessary for their own metabolism. The amounts of all sweeteners have been kept to a bare minimum here and throughout all the recipes in the book.

Most of the fruits used are high in Vitamin C and carotenoids, particularly summer fruits. The proteins and fats taken with them – crème fraîche, fromage frais, *mascarpone, ricotta, yogurts etc. – all slow the absorption of sugars.*

JM

RHUBARB WITH BLOOD ORANGES, OPAL BASIL AND MASCARPONE

SERVES 4

THE RHUBARB
300g rhubarb, cut into 12 x 6cm sticks
50g fructose

THE BLOOD ORANGES
grated zest of 3 unsprayed blood oranges
segments and juice from the cores of the 3 oranges
12 fresh opal basil leaves, finely sliced
10g fructose

THE MASCARPONE
160g mascarpone cheese
30g fructose
6 fresh opal basil leaves, finely sliced
juice and grated zest of 1 unsprayed blood orange

TO SERVE
4 fresh opal basil leaves

Method

The rhubarb
Mix the rhubarb and fructose together in a saucepan that just holds them. Cover with water to the level of the rhubarb. Bring to the boil then lower the heat. Poach the rhubarb at just below simmering point for 6 minutes, turning it once. Once cooked, gently remove the rhubarb from its liquor and place on a tray. Set aside. Place the cooking liquor back over a high heat and reduce it rapidly until it is thick and syrupy. Leave to cool.

The blood oranges
Mix all of the ingredients together. Add to the reduced rhubarb cooking liquor.

Following page:
Rhubarb with blood
oranges, opal basil
and mascarpone

The mascarpone and serving
Mix all the mascarpone ingredients together. Refrigerate until needed.

Place three pieces of rhubarb in each of four bowls. Spoon the orange segments and juice over and around. Top with the mascarpone and basil leaves.

POACHED CHERRIES WITH MAPLE SYRUP AND ROASTED ALMOND ICE-CREAM

SERVES 4

Planning ahead
Both elements of this dish may be made up to 1 day in advance.

600g black cherries, stoned
100ml maple syrup
200ml water
1 cinnamon stick

THE ICE-CREAM
100g almonds (in their brown skins)
125ml maple syrup
4 free-range egg yolks
250ml milk
50ml whipping cream

Method

The cherries
Mix the cherries in a small saucepan with the maple syrup, water and cinnamon stick. Place over a high heat and bring to the boil. Boil rapidly for $1\frac{1}{2}$ minutes then take the pan off the heat and remove the cinnamon stick. Set aside.

The ice-cream
In a small frying pan toast the almonds, tossing constantly over a medium heat for 5 minutes until golden brown. Add 3 tbsp of the maple syrup and caramelise slightly. Transfer to an oiled tray and separate them (the caramel will make them stick together slightly). Keep 12 to one side for decoration. Then coarsely chop the remainder.

Whisk the egg yolks together with the remaining maple syrup. Bring the milk to the boil then pour it slowly over the top of the egg yolks. Pour this mixture back into the saucepan and cook it over a medium heat, stirring constantly, until it coats the back of a spoon. Strain through a fine sieve, add the whipping cream and chopped caramelised almonds then cool over ice. When cold, churn in an ice-cream machine or freeze, stirring frequently, until needed.

Serving

Divide the cherries and cooking liquor between four plates and place a large ball of the ice-cream in the centre. Top with the reserved whole caramelised almonds and serve.

RB's notes

The ice-cream custard is one of those recipes that you see for the first time and think, what is meant by covering the back of a spoon? Well, the custard is cooked when it reaches 82°C/180°F, so if you have a thermometer use it. If not, the mixture is cooked when it forms a coating over the back of your wooden spoon thick enough that you can run your finger down the centre and the line that is left stays.

If you do not have an ice-cream machine, you can still make the ice-cream by placing it in a container in the freezer and stirring it regularly as it freezes. This will not achieve as smooth a texture as the machine, as the ice-cream will freeze in larger particles, but it will still be very pleasant.

GRATIN OF FIGS WITH MASCARPONE

Nutritional note

Figs not only provide carbohydrate and, famously, plenty of fibre, but also, being seeded fruit, some essential fat. The egg yolk and cheese provide fat and protein, and the lemon Vitamin C.

SERVES 4

12 fat ripe figs
100g mascarpone cheese
6 tbsp fructose
3 free-range egg yolks
juice of 1 unsprayed lemon

Method

Preheat the grill to its highest setting.

Cut each fig into about 5 slices and arrange them around the insides of four deep plates.

Mix the mascarpone with 4 tbsp of the fructose, the egg yolks and the lemon juice. Spoon this over the tops of the figs then sprinkle over the remaining fructose. Place under the preheated grill until the surfaces are golden brown. Serve immediately.

GRILLED FIGS WITH RASPBERRIES AND PORT

SERVES 4

Fresh figs are becoming more easily available in this country, the best coming from Greece and Italy.

Planning ahead
As this dish is well suited to being served either cold, warm or at room temperature, you could easily prepare it a day in advance.

12 large black figs, halved
250ml ruby port
2 large punnets (approx. 400g in total) blackberries or raspberries
4 tsp olive oil
2 tbsp fructose

Method
Put the port in a large pan and simmer to reduce by just over half. Add the blackberries, remove from the heat, and leave to macerate for an hour or so.

Mix the figs in a small bowl with the olive oil and fructose. Leave for an hour or so.

Heat a griddle or the grill, and grill the figs for 2 minutes each side over/under a medium heat.

Add the figs to the blackberries, and serve.

Variations
Grilling the figs may seem a little unusual, but it is a lovely way to concentrate the flavours as well as being a simple alternative to poaching or roasting. The method also works wonderfully well with stone fruit such as peaches and nectarines.

If you were to serve this dish warm, a ball of vanilla ice-cream would be a nice last-minute addition.

PINEAPPLE AND BLUEBERRIES WITH CHICKPEA PANCAKES

SERVES 4

Planning ahead
The pancakes may be made a day in advance and kept with the pineapple, blueberries and syrup until needed.

1 recipe *Chickpea Pancakes* (see page 40)

THE PINEAPPLE AND BLUEBERRIES
1 large pineapple (approx. 1kg, peeled)
200g blueberries
2 tbsp unsalted butter
6 tbsp maple syrup
150ml water

TO SERVE
160g ricotta cheese

Method

The pancakes
Make as described on page 40.

The pineapple and blueberries
Cut half of the pineapple into small chunks, liquidise them, then strain through a fine sieve. Set aside.

Cut the other half into 4 slices lengthways, then each of these slices into 5 triangles. Heat a frying pan with butter until foaming, add the chunks of pineapple and sauté over a medium heat for $1\frac{1}{2}$ minutes each side. Add the maple syrup and allow to caramelise slightly.

Pour in the water and boil for 1 minute, then add the pineapple purée and the blueberries. Bring back to the boil, remove from the heat and reserve.

Serving
Reheat the pineapple and blueberries. Soak the pancakes in the juices, then place 1 on each of four plates. Spread a little of the ricotta on this, then top with the pineapple chunks, blueberries and syrup. Serve immediately.

CONFIT OF PLUMS IN RED WINE WITH VANILLA

This is a dish that my mother gave us as children in the days when you wouldn't even consider eating a plum unless it had fallen from the tree on its own (or you'd had the excitement of stealing it from your grumpy neighbour's orchard). Alas, things have changed but if you take the trouble you can still find some wonderful organic plums and I salute my time in England by having a big dollop of clotted cream to accompany them.

Nutritional note

Plums, from the *Prunus* family (as are cherries and peaches), contain many vitamins and minerals when ripe and dark. With the small amount of fructose added for sweetening, they will provide the carbohydrate required for correct utilisation of the protein in any main course.

SERVES 4

Planning ahead

No problems here: the *confit* can be made up to 3 days in advance and kept refrigerated.

8 of the blackest, ripest plums you can find (approx. 800g), halved and stoned, each half sliced in 4
300ml red wine
40g fructose
1 vanilla pod, split

TO SERVE

200g clotted cream

Method

Reduce the wine by half by boiling, then add the fructose, the plums and the vanilla pod and scraped seeds. Bring this mixture to the boil and simmer for 10 minutes until the plums are soft but have not dissolved. Remove from the heat and set aside. (Take out the vanilla pod, wash and dry it then reserve for another use.)

Divide the plums between four bowls and place a spoonful of clotted cream in the centre. The plums can be served either hot or cold.

Variations

If you are lucky enough to be able to procure them, this could be prepared using 'black' peaches. Cherries would also be very pleasant. Cooked a bit longer, with a slightly higher percentage of fructose, you could make a delicious and original jam.

If you are not quite the hedonist that I am, you can replace the clotted cream with whipping or single cream.

ROASTED PEACHES WITH PEACH AND LAVENDER COULIS

Here the peach is really the star. Slowly roasted in the oven, its flavours concentrate wonderfully. The *coulis*, with the addition of lavender, evokes the aromas of Provence.

SERVES 4

Planning ahead
This is a dish which is equally good served hot or at room temperature so you can prepare it a day in advance and reheat it.

4 large ripe peaches
20g unsalted butter
20g fructose

THE *COULIS*
2 large ripe peaches, approx. 300g, stoned and cut into small dice
10g unsalted butter
20g fructose
50ml dry white wine
2 stalks of fresh lavender, flowers picked

Method

The peaches
Preheat the oven to 160°C/325°F/Gas 3. Make a small incision in the top of each peach, place them on a little ovenproof tray and top each with a little of the butter. Sprinkle the fructose over them, then roast in the preheated oven for 30 minutes. Peel the peaches and keep warm.

The *coulis*
Heat a small frying pan with the butter until it begins to foam. Add the peach dice and fry for 2 minutes over a high heat. Spoon in the fructose then, stirring frequently so that the peaches do not catch, cook for a further minute. Add the white wine, bring it to the boil and allow it to reduce by half, about 1 minute.

Transfer from the pan to the bowl of a liquidiser and purée with the lavender flowers until totally fine. Set aside.

Serving
Pour the *coulis* into the bases of four bowls, and top with the roasted peaches. Pour the roasting juices over and serve.

FIGS AND STRAWBERRIES WITH BALSAMIC VINEGAR

SERVES 4

As with all very simple recipes, the success of this relies solely on the freshness and quality of the ingredients used.

16 large purple figs
40 strawberries
4 tbsp balsamic vinegar (the older the better)
4 tsp fructose

Method

Preheat the oven to 180°C/350°F/Gas 4.

Cut the figs into 4 and hull the strawberries. Place them all into an ovenproof dish, pour over the vinegar and about the same amount of water, and sprinkle with the fructose. Bake in the oven for 10 minutes.

Serve as is or with a dollop of *crème fraîche* or mascarpone cheese.

PINK GRAPEFRUIT IN CAMPARI WITH MASCARPONE SORBET

SERVES 4

Planning ahead
Both the grapefruit and the sorbet may be prepared about 12 hours before serving.

4 large unsprayed pink grapefruit
40g fructose
4 tbsp Campari

THE SORBET
250g mascarpone cheese
100g fructose
350ml water
juice of 1 unsprayed lemon

Method
Peel the grapefruit with a small sharp knife, removing all traces of skin and pith. Working over the top of a bowl so that you catch any juice that escapes, remove all of the segments and squeeze the cores to catch the remaining juice. Add the fructose and the Campari to the segments and juice, then refrigerate.

For the sorbet, boil together the fructose and water. Allow this syrup to cool then whisk into the mascarpone. Acidulate slightly with the lemon juice, then pour into a sorbet machine and freeze. (If you don't have one, place it in a bowl in the freezer and stir it as often as possible while it freezes.)

To serve, put the grapefruit segments and juice into bowls and top with the sorbet.

Variations
The grapefruit may be replaced with oranges or, in season, with blood oranges.

ROASTED BANANAS WITH LYCHEES AND PASSIONFRUIT

SERVES 4

4 medium ripe bananas
20ml groundnut oil
30g palm sugar

THE PASSIONFRUIT SALAD

pulp of 6 passionfruit
8 lychees, peeled and stoned
50ml water
30–40g palm sugar (depending on the acidity of the passionfruit)

TO SERVE

40g creamed coconut, grated
6 fresh lemon verbena leaves, finely sliced

Method

The roasted bananas

Peel the bananas and slice each into five pieces at a slant.

Heat a frying pan with the groundnut oil, add the bananas, and fry them for 1 minute until golden. Add the palm sugar, lower the heat, and fry for a further 2 minutes until the bananas are well caramelised. Transfer them very gently from the pan on to a tray and set aside.

The passionfruit salad

Mix the pulp and seeds of the passionfruit with the lychees, water and palm sugar. Set aside.

Serving

Arrange the roasted bananas around the outside of four plates. Place the lychees in the centre and top them with the grated coconut. Pour the passionfruit juice around and over the bananas. Sprinkle with the lemon verbena and serve.

STRAWBERRIES WITH RHUBARB AND RICOTTA

SERVES 4

Planning ahead
The rhubarb may be cooked up to a day in advance and the strawberry and ricotta mixtures may be made half a day before serving.

THE RHUBARB
300g rhubarb, well washed and cut in 3cm diamonds
60g fructose

THE STRAWBERRIES
200g strawberries, hulled and halved
juice of 1 unsprayed orange
fructose to taste

THE RICOTTA
160g ricotta cheese
4 large strawberries, finely sliced
fructose to taste

Method

The rhubarb
Place the rhubarb in a saucepan that just holds it, just cover with water, and add the fructose. Bring to the boil then turn the heat down as low as possible and poach until soft, about 6 minutes, turning once during the cooking time. Do not be tempted to stir too much as the rhubarb pieces will turn to purée. Leave to cool in the cooking liquor.

The strawberries and ricotta
Liquidise 100g of the halved strawberries in a blender with the orange juice, then add the remaining strawberries to this. Sweeten to taste with the fructose. Reserve.

For the ricotta, simply mix the ingredients together and sweeten to taste.

Serving
Arrange the halved strawberries and pieces of drained rhubarb around the outsides of four deep plates. Pour the strawberry juice over and place a ball of ricotta in the centre.

Variations

Exactly the same dish may be made with raspberries or blackberries, the only difference being that you will need to sieve the purée, and you will probably need a little more fructose. If you have the good fortune to get them, the most wonderful variation would be with wild strawberries.

STRAWBERRIES AND RASPBERRIES WITH CREAM

SERVES 4

500g strawberries
250g raspberries
100g goat's milk cream (optional)
50g fructose

Method

Purée half of the fruit with the goat's milk cream and half of the fructose. Quarter or halve the remaining strawberries, and mix with the remaining raspberries and fructose. Mix in with the fruit purée. Serve in large bowls.

CARAMELISED APPLES IN SPICED WINE

SERVES 4

Planning ahead
This dessert benefits from being marinated so, as long as it is heated gently before serving, it may be made a day in advance.

4 large Granny Smith or Bramley apples, each peeled, cored and cut into
  8 segments
100g fructose
40g unsalted butter
250ml full-bodied red wine
1 vanilla pod, halved and scraped
1 cinnamon stick
1 small unsprayed orange, cut into 12 very thin slices, skin on
20 Cape gooseberries, husked

Method
Sprinkle the fructose over the base of a large, preferably non-stick, frying pan and place it over a high heat for about 3 minutes until the fructose turns a dark caramel colour. Add the butter and combine well.

Place the apple segments in a single layer into the pan and caramelise over a medium heat for 3–4 minutes until soft but still holding their shape. Remove the pan from the heat and set aside.

In a saucepan, bring the red wine to the boil and allow to boil for 3 minutes. Add the vanilla, cinnamon, orange slices and gooseberries. Bring back to the boil, then add to the pan with the caramelised apples. Heat slightly so that you dissolve all of the caramel in the pan then transfer to a large bowl.

Allow to marinate for at least 2 hours, then serve, still slightly warm.

Variations
This would be very pleasant served with cinnamon or vanilla ice-cream.

POACHED PEACHES WITH LEMONGRASS SYRUP

SERVES 4

Planning ahead
The peaches may be poached well ahead of serving as the syrup is best as cold as possible.

8 very ripe peaches
450g fructose
1 litre water
4 lemongrass stalks, finely chopped
2 tbsp coriander seeds, crushed
grated zest of 1 unsprayed orange, 1 lemon and 1 lime

Method
Bring the fructose, water, lemongrass and coriander seeds to the boil. Add the peaches and cover with a piece of greaseproof paper. Poach the peaches at just below simmering point for 10–15 minutes, depending on their ripeness. Make sure that during the cooking time they remain totally submerged.

Once cooked, add the citrus zests to the syrup and leave the peaches to cool.

To serve, simply place the peaches into a bowl and strain some of the cooking liquor over the top.

BAKED TAMARILLOS WITH HAZELNUT CRÈME ANGLAISE

This fruit, which I have only recently begun to use, is otherwise known as the tree tomato. It has a very interesting, slightly acidic flavour that marries well with the honey.

SERVES 4

Planning ahead

The *crème anglaise* may be made a day or so in advance.

8 large tamarillos
4 tsp liquid honey

THE *CRÈME ANGLAISE*

7 tbsp fructose
300ml milk
100g unskinned hazelnuts, roughly chopped
5 large free-range egg yolks

Method

To make the *crème anglaise*, place the hazelnuts into a small pan and toast them over a medium heat for 3–4 minutes. Add 2 tbsp of the fructose and caramelise lightly for about a minute. Add the milk and bring to the boil.

Whisk the egg yolks together with the remaining 5 tbsp fructose until pale, then slowly pour the milk on to them, whisking continuously. Pour this mixture back into the saucepan and cook it over a medium heat, stirring constantly until it coats the back of a spoon (see page 271). Transfer to a bowl over another of ice and stir frequently until totally cold. Reserve in the fridge.

To cook the tamarillos, preheat the oven to 200°C/400°F/Gas 6.

Slit the tops of the tamarillos and blanch for 30 seconds in plenty of boiling water. Transfer to cold water and then peel in the same manner that you would a tomato. Place in an ovenproof dish, coat with the honey and bake for 10 minutes.

Serve the baked tamarillos in deep bowls on top of the hazelnut *crème anglaise*.

MELON SOUP WITH RED WINE GRANITA

Colourful and fresh, just the thing for a languid summer evening.

SERVES 4

Planning ahead
Both the soup and *granita* can be made a full day in advance.

  1 very large, very ripe cantaloupe melon
  500ml water
  5 tbsp fructose
  juice of 1 unsprayed lime
  8 fresh mint leaves, finely sliced

THE RED WINE *GRANITA*
300ml red wine
80g fructose
grated zest of 1 unsprayed lemon and 1 unsprayed orange

Method
Wash the melon very well. Peel it, and chop the skin finely. Halve the melon then place the seeds and filament with the skin into a pan. Cut the melon flesh into thin slices and set aside in a bowl. Cover the skin and seeds with the water and add the fructose. Bring the mixture to the boil, skim and simmer for 15 minutes. Pour this through a sieve over the melon, then set aside. When it is cold, add the lime juice and finely sliced mint.

To make the *granita*, boil the red wine with the fructose, then add the zests. Simmer for 2 minutes, then strain and freeze.

Distribute the melon and soup between four bowls. Grate the red wine *granita* over the top and serve.

BAKED PEARS WITH ALMONDS AND HONEY

SERVES 4

4 large, very ripe pears (Williams and Comice are the best)
2 tsp liquid honey
2 tsp fructose
60g whole unskinned almonds
$\frac{1}{2}$ cinnamon stick, finely grated (use a grater or mortar and pestle)

Method

Preheat the oven to 200°C/400°F/Gas 6.

Cut each pear into 6 and remove the cores. Place the pieces in an ovenproof tray with the honey, fructose, almonds and cinnamon, then into the preheated oven for 10 minutes.

Serve immediately.

Variation

A nice touch with the pears would be a spoonful of vanilla or cinnamon ice-cream.

RB's note

This dish depends totally on the quality of your pears, so choose carefully. If you can't find good ones, make something else.

MANDARINS AND GOOSEBERRIES IN THEIR OWN JUICES

SERVES 4

Planning ahead
The entire preparation may be done a good day in advance.

    4 tsp liquid honey
    4 tbsp fructose
    1 medium unsprayed orange, cut in 12 very fine slices
    juice of 8 mandarin oranges
    4 mandarin oranges, peeled and segmented
    48 Cape gooseberries, husks removed
    50g almonds, sliced

Method
Place the honey and fructose in a large flat pan over a medium heat until they melt (don't let them colour). Add the orange slices and cook for about 2 minutes on each side. Add the mandarin juice and boil for a minute. Add the mandarin segments and gooseberries, and toss well.

Transfer to a bowl, allow to cool and serve, sprinkled with the almonds.

RB's note
The mandarin segments may be replaced by orange segments.

LEMON VERBENA CREAMS WITH LEMON SYRUP

Nutritional note

Vegetarians who are not vegans will benefit from the good protein of eggs and milk in this dish. This pudding is excellent because it does not have a high glycaemic index, despite being sweet.

SERVES 4

Planning ahead

The creams need to be made a few hours in advance, and can be made up to a day before serving, as can the syrup.

500ml milk
70g fructose
1 large bunch of fresh lemon verbena, leaves picked and finely sliced
6 free-range egg yolks

THE LEMON SYRUP

2 unsprayed lemons
2 tbsp water
30g fructose

Method

Preheat the oven to 180°C/350°F/Gas 4.

The creams

Mix the milk and fructose together in a saucepan then bring to the boil. Add the sliced lemon verbena, and allow to cool. Mix the fragrant milk with the egg yolks, then strain through your finest sieve.

Prepare a *bain-marie*, so that the water comes two-thirds of the way up the sides of your ramekins or moulds. Place a piece of kitchen paper over the bottom of this so that the moulds won't slip, then pour the mixture into them. Cover the *bain-marie* with a piece of foil, then place in the preheated oven for 15 minutes. Turn the oven down to 160°C/325°F/Gas 3, remove the foil and allow to cook for a further 20 minutes. They should still be relatively sloppy in the centre. This will give you a much softer and creamier texture once the creams have cooled, and a less obvious taste of egg. Transfer to a container of cold water to cool. Once cold, reserve well clingfilmed until needed.

The lemon syrup and serving

Finely grate the zest of the 2 lemons, then squeeze the juice from 1, and segment the other. Boil together the lemon zest and juice with the water and fructose. When this takes on a syrupy consistency, remove it from the heat and add the lemon segments. Simply spoon the syrup and lemon segments over the tops of the creams in their moulds.

CHOCOLATE POT À LA CRÈME

SERVES 4

Planning ahead
As *Lemon Verbena Creams* (see page 292).

500ml milk
20g cocoa powder
100g fructose
100g bitter chocolate, grated
6 free-range egg yolks

Method
Preheat the oven to 180°C/350°F/Gas 4.

Mix the milk, cocoa powder and fructose together in a saucepan then bring to the boil. Add the chocolate, stir in well until it melts, then allow to cool.

Mix with the egg yolks then strain the chocolate milk through your finest sieve. Prepare a *bain-marie*, as in the *Lemon Verbena Creams* recipe (see page 292), and cook the chocolate pots exactly as described there. Once cold, reserve well clingfilmed until needed.

COFFEE AND CARAMEL POT À LA CRÈME

SERVES 4

Planning ahead
As *Lemon Verbena Creams* (see page 292).

500ml milk
80g dark coffee beans, well crushed
100g fructose
6 free-range egg yolks

Method
Preheat the oven to 180°C/350°F/Gas 4.

Heat the milk and set aside.

Roast the crushed coffee beans in the bottom of a small saucepan. Add the fructose and cook to a dark caramel. Add the warmed milk to this and bring back to the boil. Allow to cool.

Mix this coffee milk with the egg yolks, then strain through your finest sieve. Prepare a *bain-marie*, as in the *Lemon Verbena Creams* recipe on page 292, and cook the coffee and caramel pots exactly as described there.

CHOCOLATE AND RASPBERRY TORTE

SERVES 8

Planning ahead
The *torte* may be made about 8 hours in advance, but should be kept at room temperature.

150g bitter chocolate, grated
50g unsalted butter, cut into cubes
50ml whipping cream
7 free-range eggs, separated
50g fructose
30g chickpea flour
40g cocoa powder
250g raspberries

Method
Preheat the oven to 180°C/350°F/Gas 4.

Grease a 22cm cake tin with extra butter, sprinkle with extra cocoa, then place on a baking sheet.

Melt the chocolate over a pan of barely simmering water or in the microwave on its lowest setting. Stir in the butter, piece by piece, followed by the cream, then remove from the heat.

In a mixing bowl whisk the egg whites until they reach soft peaks, adding the fructose gradually. Stir in the egg yolks and sprinkle in the flour and cocoa powder. Fold in the chocolate and butter mixture slowly with a spatula.

Pour half of the mixture into the prepared tin then sprinkle half of the raspberries evenly over it. Top with the remaining mixture and then the remaining raspberries. Bake the *torte* in the preheated oven for 30–35 minutes until the blade of a small knife comes out of the centre almost dry. Transfer the torte to a cooling rack and leave to cool.

Serve either on its own or with a raspberry purée (raspberries puréed and sieved, sweetened to taste with a little fructose and spiked with a dash of lemon juice).

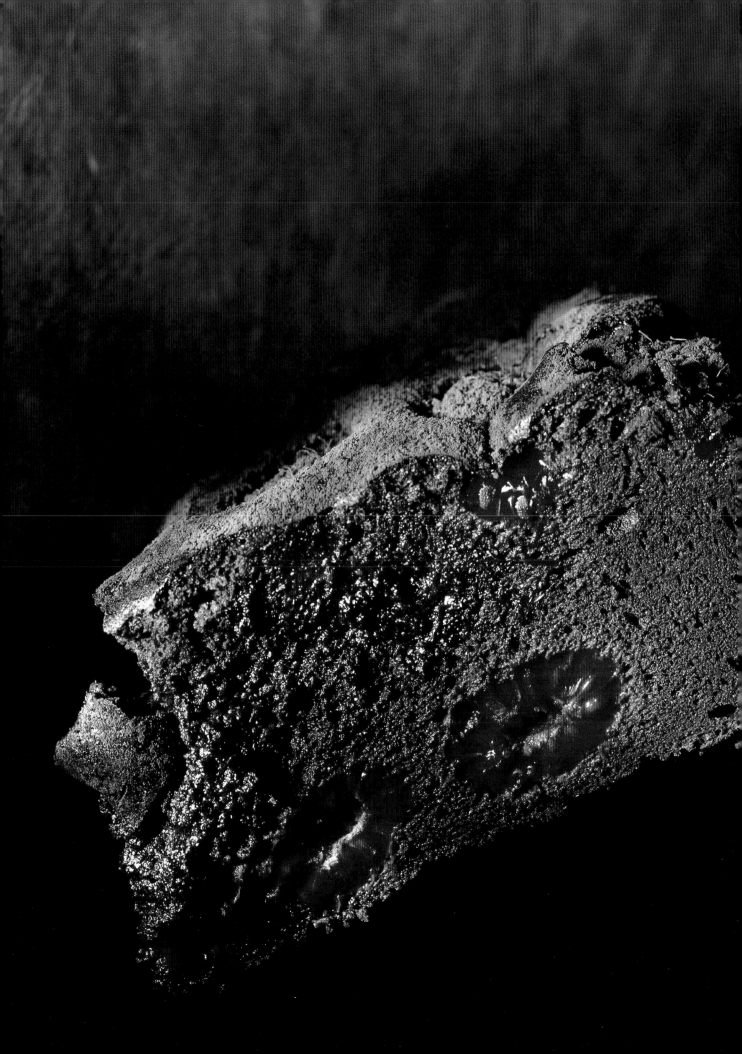

CHOCOLATE MOUSSE

SERVES 4

Nutritional note

The 70% cocoa solids content makes this chocolate dish excellent, especially for children (and chocoholics). Most chocolate has been adulterated with flavourings and additives, which debase it. Despite the fructose, this is not a high glycaemic dish.

Planning ahead
Can be prepared one day in advance.

150g dark chocolate (70% cocoa solids), broken into squares
20g unsweetened cocoa powder
20ml warm water
1 free-range egg yolk
4 free-range egg whites
20g fructose

Method
Melt the chocolate in a bowl over a pan of hot water. While the chocolate is melting mix the cocoa powder with the warm water and then the egg yolk. Add this to the melted chocolate then set aside.

Whip the egg whites to soft peaks, add the fructose, then whip to stiff peaks.

Vigorously mix a third of the egg white into the chocolate then gently fold in the remainder. Place in four ramekins and refrigerate for a minimum of an hour.

OEUFS À LA NEIGE

SERVES 4

Planning ahead
Both the *crème anglaise* and the snow eggs may be made half a day in advance.

750ml milk
1 vanilla pod, split lengthways
6 free-range egg whites
300g fructose
8 free-range egg yolks

Method
Bring the milk to the boil with the vanilla pod. Keep warm over the lowest possible heat.

In an electric mixer on medium speed, beat the egg whites to soft peaks, then add 175g of the fructose little by little. When all in, increase the speed and beat until firm.

Scoop out 8 large spoonfuls of meringue, and poach 4 at a time for 2 minutes on each side in the milk at just below simmering point, turning them very gently with a slotted spoon. Remove them and allow to drain on a tray lined with absorbent paper.

Whisk the egg yolks together with the remaining fructose in a bowl, and pour in the poaching milk. Whisk together well, then return to a clean saucepan over a medium heat. Stir continuously until the mixture coats the back of a spoon. Strain immediately into a clean bowl and leave to cool and 'set'. Add the poached meringues to the bowl then refrigerate for at least 4 hours.

Serve at the table for everyone to help themselves.

APPENDICES
I SUPERFOODS

These are foods which have natural health-giving and even medicinal effects. As stated before, most foods can be eaten for health, so long as they are unrefined and produced in an organic way, so most foods are Superfoods to some extent.

CHOCOLATE

Chocolate and cocoa powder come from the pods of the tropical tree, *Theobroma cacao*. Despite its relatively high content of saturated fatty acids, chocolate can contribute a significant amount of dietary antioxidants and bioflavonoids. The caffeine content can in excess produce palpitations and other side-effects, but in ordinary consumption, chocolate can improve mental performance, memory, alertness and feelings of well-being, and delay physical fatigue. Chocolate is a major source of dietary copper, contains significant amounts of manganese and magnesium, and cocoa can be used in zinc deficiency.

DAIRY PRODUCTS

Dairy products – milk, butter, cheese, eggs and yogurt etc. – are a rich source of calcium, phosphorus and selenium. They also contain saturated fat. **Milk** is a source of zinc and organic **butter** of Vitamin A. **Eggs** are a good protein source, and are a complete food, lacking only Vitamin C (which most species can make for themselves, but not man). They contain copper, iodine and iron. Egg yolk is a rich source of folate and zinc. **Yogurt** is an excellent protein, which is very easily digestible, because the lactobacilli (bacteria) have 'pre-digested' the lactose (milk sugars). Live bio yogurt can be useful in many ways. The lactobacilli are protective against infectious diseases in the gut and cancer of the colon, and can help when intestinal flora have been disrupted by a course of antibiotics.

FRUIT

All fruits contain good carbohydrate and many fibrous components for effective intestinal transit. They are also rich in minerals and vitamins, and are amongst the most important vital elements for health. Red and yellow fruits in particular contain carotenoids, among them **apricots**, **cherries**, **citrus fruit**, **melons**, **papaya** (pawpaw) and **mango**. Fruits also contain bioflavonoids, in particular **apples**, **apricots**, **cherries**, **citrus fruits**, **grapes** and all the **summer fruits**. Most fruits are rich in Vitamin C, particularly **blackberries**, **blackcurrants**, **citrus fruit**, **guavas**, and **kiwi fruit**. **Figs** are rich in fibre, and **bananas** are good sources of potassium, magnesium and fibre. **Dried fruits** have excellent quantities of fibre and iron; **sultanas**, particularly the darker varieties, contain all the components of red wine (see page 304), as the skins are intact. **Pineapple** is a source of iodine and selenium, and contains an enzyme, bromelain, which is a protein-digester, and is said to be useful in a number of ways, combating infection and inflammation; it has also been used in the treatment of cancer. **Papaya** contains a similar enzyme, papain. **Rhubarb** may help to heal gastric ulcers.

FUNGI AND YEAST

Yeast is a rich source of folate and Vitamin B6 when cooked. **Mushrooms**, both cultivated and wild, contain chromium, copper and pantothenic acid, a B vitamin. Shiitake mushrooms are said to be protective against cancer, especially of the breast.

GRAINS

Whole grains have not been refined or adulterated. They may have been processed in some way – by milling, rolling or flaking – but nothing should have been extracted and nothing added. Whole grains are good sources of carbohydrate, particularly fibre and vitamins, including the B vitamins, copper, manganese, iodine, selenium and magnesium, and together with legumes or pulses (or other dietary components) can provide complete proteins. Food made from whole grains – pasta etc. – contain the same nutrients. **Buckwheat** is a good source of bioflavonoids, **corn** of zinc. **Oats** are naturally cholesterol-lowering. **Brown rice** is rich in Vitamin E and B vitamins, including niacin (nicotinic acid), which are helpful in the metabolism of the rice. **Whole wheat** is a rich source of Vitamin B6 and niacin; the bran contains niacin, Vitamin B6 and folate; the germ has B1, B6 and folate.

HERBS AND SPICES

Herbs and spices are often the richest sources of aromatic compounds and essential oils, bioflavonoids and minerals.

Basil is reputedly helpful for migraine, nervous tension, constipation and insomnia. It is a natural disinfectant. **Bay leaves** help stimulate appetite and aid digestion. **Cardamom** is a natural diuretic and can help digestion. **Chervil** is rich in Vitamin C, iron, magnesium and beta-carotene. It acts as a diuretic and benefits the liver; it's good for treating gout, rheumatism and eye troubles. **Chives**, being a member of the Allium family (see **Onions**), share many of the Allium properties, and also stimulate appetite and aid digestion. **Cinnamon** is useful in treating some gynaecological conditions and suppressing some viral infections. It contains chromium, which helps the body to use sugars. **Coriander**, herb and seeds, combines sedative and stimulant effects; the seeds if chewed are an aid to digestion. **Cumin** is a good general tonic, and is antiseptic and antibacterial.

Dill, herb and seeds, can be stimulant and sedative, and is digestive, often used in the treatment of infant colic. **Fennel** has many medicinal properties, and is diuretic, tonic and sedative; it is particularly effective in digestion, very good with fish. **Fenugreek** contains carotenes, and can improve glucose tolerance in diabetics.

Garlic contains active sulphur compounds, alliins, as do the rest of the Allium family (see Onions), that are widely believed to protect against cancer and cardiovascular disease. It is a natural antiseptic and antibiotic, can lower cholesterol in the bloodstream, lower blood pressure, and enhance the immune system.

Ginger, a rhizome spice, is available fresh, dried and powdered, is warming and carminative (relieving intestinal gas, relaxing and soothing the gastrointestinal tract). It is anti-inflammatory, and analgesic, used in the treatment of rheumatism and arthritis.

Horseradish is a member of the Cruciferae (cabbage) family, and is pungent (like mustard); it is an excellent digestive, stimulant of salivary and other digestive juices. Lavender is diuretic, calming for nervous diseases of the stomach, and stress. Lemon balm is said to cure many nervous afflictions. Lemongrass has been used as an antiseptic, a sedative (reducing anxiety and promoting sleep) and digestive. Lovage seeds, leaves and roots may be beneficial for rheumatism, and the leaves are good for treating urinary problems and jaundice. Marjoram is an excellent digestive, and mint is antispasmodic and carminative. Mustard, containing active compounds similar to horseradish, is also a crucifer; it is an excellent digestive, can help joint pains and problems of the chest and lungs, and can have anti-cancer properties. Oregano is sedative and calming, and a good diuretic.

Parsley is rich in Vitamins A, B and C and many of the other nutrients of green leaves, notably iron and calcium. It is a natural antiseptic and diuretic. Rocket, used as both salad leaf and herb, is a recognised antiscorbutic because of its Vitamin C content. For medicinal purposes, the plant is most effective when gathered while still in flower. Rosemary is a very rich source of many bioflavonoids, and has many medicinal qualities; it is diuretic and stimulant, and can assist with stress. Saffron contains carotenoids. Sage is a natural antiseptic, tonic and stimulant. It is also antispasmodic and an antidote to fatigue, and aids in the digestion of rich and fatty foods. Sorrel is rich in potassium and Vitamins A, B and C. It has a high oxalic acid content, so should be avoided by people suffering from gout, rheumatism or arthritis. The leaves may be used as a diuretic, tonic or mild laxative. Savory aids digestion and is diuretic.

Tarragon acts as a stimulant and calmant at the same time, aiding digestion. Thyme is a natural antiseptic because of its high thymol (essential oil) content; it is also diuretic and digestive. Turmeric is a powerful antioxidant. Watercress is rich in iron, Vitamin C and other minerals. It is effective in combating bronchial problems, protective against lung cancer, and stimulates the circulation.

MEAT, POULTRY AND GAME

The meat of animals, poultry and game is the principal source in the human diet of complete protein, and is a good provider of many B vitamins and minerals; lean meat, for example, is a good source of manganese, potassium and selenium; red meats (beef, lamb, pork, venison) contain a lot of iron. Offal, especially liver, is a good source of iron, copper and iodine, and is rich in B vitamins. All meats contain saturated fat. Game is often lower in this than farmed livestock.

Absorption of copper from goose liver (*foie gras*) is higher than from goose meat; women are able to absorb far more copper from goose liver than from other sources of foods.

NUTS AND SEEDS

Nuts and seeds contain incomplete protein, essential fats, many nutrients and vitamins. The same applies to the oils pressed from them. In the diet, their fats help to slow absorption of sugars. Almonds are rich in protein, essential fats and some of the vital B vitamins. They are also good sources of zinc, magnesium, potassium and iron. Brazil nuts and chestnuts are rich in Vitamin B1. Coconut has rich fats, but these are well digested, as the flesh contains minerals to assist with its own metabolism. Hazelnuts are a rich source of Vitamin B6. Pine kernels contain essential oils as do peanuts (B1 and niacin too) and pumpkin seeds. Sesame seeds are rich in Vitamin E and essential fats, and contain a sulphur-rich amino acid which is a useful protein source. Sunflower seeds are rich in niacin and Vitamin B6. (Sprouted seeds are healthier still, containing Vitamins B1, B2 and C; alfalfa sprouts have E as well, and are reputed to reduce cholesterol significantly.) **Walnuts**, particularly those grown in the West, are a good source of Vitamins E and B (young green fruits contain C).

OILS

Organic and cold-pressed oils are a good source of essential fatty acids and, although they contain calories, are healthy, particularly the mono-unsaturated oils such as olive oil. Most oils are rich in Vitamin E. Cold-pressed extra virgin olive oil is the very best of all for flavour and properties (it plays a huge part in the benefits of the Mediterranean diet). Keep all oils away from light so they do not denature.

PULSES

Pulses or legumes (**peas**, **chickpeas**, **beans** and **lentils**) are the dried seeds of members of the Leguminosae family, and are very nutritious because, like grains and seeds, they contain everything for the next generation of plants. They are rich in vegetable protein, which is incomplete (apart from the soya bean). They contain little fat, and are good sources of B vitamins, particularly B6 and folate, and calcium, copper, iron, potassium, magnesium and zinc. They are good dietary carbohydrate as well, providing dietary fibre which helps gastrointestinal function. Beans can lower cholesterol. **Soya beans** are as near to a complete protein as is possible in the vegetable kingdom, and possess natural oestrogen-like properties which help symptoms of the menopause and may help protect against cancer of the breast.

All pulses, apart from lentils, contain toxic substances which must be inactivated by correct cooking.

SEAFOOD

Fish and shellfish are high protein foods. They also contain fat-soluble vitamins, many minerals (particularly iodine, phosphorus and sodium), and essential fatty acids. **Canned fish** with edible bones are a rich source of calcium. **Oily fish** and **oysters** are rich in B vitamins, iron and zinc. **Sardines** are also rich in iron, and tuna in niacin. **Shellfish** are a good source of chromium and copper.

VEGETABLES

All vegetables contain good carbohydrate and many fibrous components for effective intestinal transit. They are also rich in minerals and vitamins, and are amongst the most vital elements for health. Red and yellow vegetables in particular contain carotenoids, among them **beetroot**, **carrots**, **sweet** and **chilli peppers**, **pumpkins** and **squashes**, **sweet potatoes** and **tomatoes**. The darker green and leafy vegetables also contain rich nutrients, particularly Vitamins A and C; **spinach**, for instance, is a rich source of calcium, copper, iron, magnesium and bioflavonoids. **Artichokes** can help balance intestinal flora, and asparagus contains an active compound which is beneficial for the liver and kidneys. The dark skin of **aubergines** contains bioflavonoids which can prevent the formation of 'plaque' in blood vessels, and hence reduces angina and the risk of stroke. It can also help to lower cholesterol. **Fresh beans** contain many of the principles of their dried counterparts, as well as Vitamin C.

The cabbage (Cruciferae) family includes **red** and **green cabbage, broccoli, Brussels sprouts, cauliflower** and **kale**, all of which contain Vitamin C and sulphur and are said to have anti-cancer properties. An over-usage of them can be a problem, so although they are Superfoods, they must be eaten in moderation.

Onions are rich in alliins, the active sulphur compounds in **garlic**, **leeks**, **shallots** and other members of the Allium family, and are widely believed to protect against cancer and cardiovascular disease. **Onion** also has blood sugar, blood pressure and cholesterol lowering effects. It is anti-inflammatory and enhances the immune system.

Peppers, both sweet and chilli, are rich in Vitamin C and beta-carotene. The hot oils in **chilli peppers** can be digestive, but should be used in moderation. **Potatoes** contain potassium, and good amounts of fibre in the skins. **Seaweed** contains iodine and niacin. **Tomatoes** are particularly rich in vitamins, bioflavonoids and iron, so are good for the blood and nervous system, and help protect against cancer.

WINE

Many scientific studies have been searching for the answer to the so-called 'French Paradox'. This concerns the anomaly of people in southern France and other Mediterranean countries having an incidence of coronary heart disease which is significantly lower than that in other developed countries, despite a high consumption of fat. Scientists now think that diet, in particular regular intake of red wine, is responsible for this cardio-protective effect.

All wine contains what are known as oligomeric proanthocyanidins. These contain many principles which are protective of health in a number of ways, but it is red wine that is the most significant. This is because of the skins, which in red wines are left to ferment with the crushed grapes and juices to add flavour and colour. (In white wines, fermentation takes place *after* the skins have been removed.) A substance called resveratrol is present in grape skins which is thought to contain many healthy properties: in a study the most resveratrol was found in a red French Bordeaux, the least in its white counterpart. Resveratrol has anti-clotting properties and this protects against atherosclerosis and heart disease. Other wine compounds, including flavonoids and antioxidants, are thought to protect against infection, cancer and dementia.

A friendly word of warning, though, to those tempted to hit the bottle at this point. Two to four daily glasses of red wine is the level associated with decreased incidence of disease. Moderate drinkers live longer and are less likely to die from heart disease than teetotallers, but those with a tendency to drink too much place huge strains on heart, liver and digestive tract. It is interesting and healthy to note that red grape juice has the same properties as red wine . . .

Wine in itself is not a cure-all, nor is it the only reason for the French Paradox, but it is certainly the most fun. *A votre santé.*

II VITAMINS

VITAMIN A (RETINOL, ANIMAL SOURCES) (BETA-CAROTENE, VEGETABLE SOURCES)

Important for skin and mucous membranes, helps with eyesight and may be important in the utilisation of iron by the body. It is a powerful antioxidant. Retinol, which is fat-soluble, resists most cooking processes except frying at high temperatures. It is sensitive to oxygen and light. Beta-carotene, which is water-soluble, is sensitive to light, oxygen and heat. It is converted to Vitamin A in the body.

RICHEST SOURCES

Cod liver oil, halibut liver oil, ox liver, chicken liver, lamb's liver, pumpkin, spinach, sweet potato, dried apricots, broccoli, cabbage, mature carrots, cooked carrots, cantaloupe melon, Cheddar cheese, cherries, eel, kale, papaya, mango, sweet peppers, chilli peppers, peaches, prunes, tomato, watercress, dark green leaves and herbs, watermelon, whole powdered milk, eggs, fresh apricots, organic butter.

ESPECIALLY NEEDED BY

Pregnant women (but too much can be a risk to the foetus), those who are under stress, the elderly, faddy eaters and dieters. It helps to protect mucous membranes against infections and cancer.

VITAMIN B1 (THIAMIN)

Essential for the full metabolism of carbohydrates and fats, the chief sources of bodily energy; for the proper functioning of nerve tissues, and all muscles including the heart. It aids digestion and promotes energy and growth. It is water-soluble, and is lost when food is soaked and water is discarded, when cooking water is discarded, and when meats and other foods are cooked at high temperatures.

RICHEST SOURCES

Brewer's yeast, wheatgerm, liver, peanuts, Brazil nuts, chestnuts, hazelnuts, sprouted pulses, whole grains and seeds, oats (raw), dried peas, green peas (fresh), soya flour, pork, butter, peanuts and haricot beans.

ESPECIALLY NEEDED BY

Pregnant and lactating women, women on the Pill or HRT, those indulging in high physical activity, junk-food eaters, and the elderly.

VITAMIN B2 (RIBOFLAVIN)

Essential (with other vitamins) for the synthesis of hormones by the pituitary and adrenal glands to meet stress by fight or flight, for energy production in the body, for healthy eyes, skin and hair, and plays a part in the metabolism of proteins, carbohydrates and fats. It prevents soreness of the lips, mouth and tongue. It is water-soluble, and is lost when cooking water is discarded, although fairly stable when heated. Exposure to light diminishes it (i.e. milk bottles left in sunlight on the doorstep).

RICHEST SOURCES
Kidney, liver, whole and sprouted grains, legumes and seeds, yeast extract, wheatgerm, dairy produce, green leafy vegetables.

ESPECIALLY NEEDED BY
Pregnant and lactating women, children who are growing fast, women on the Pill or HRT, and the elderly.

VITAMIN B3 (NIACIN/NICOTINIC ACID)

Prevents gastro-intestinal disturbances. Helps in energy production and blood circulation. Needed for the metabolism of fats, protein and carbohydrate. It is water-soluble, and is fairly stable in cooking, although it may be lost when cooking water is discarded.

RICHEST SOURCES
Yeast extract, dulse seaweed, kidney, liver, peanuts, poultry, sunflower and sesame seeds, oily fish, wheat bran, wheatgerm, whole brown rice, wholemeal flour, dried apricots, beans (sprouts especially), lentils, mushrooms.

ESPECIALLY NEEDED BY
Pregnant and lactating women, by children undergoing rapid growth, by those who physically exert themselves and those who are stressed.

PANTOTHENIC ACID (PANTOTHENATE)

Essential for proper functioning of the adrenal glands, helps in allergy, involved in the formation of antibodies, accelerates the healing of wounds of all kinds, and protects skin and mucous membranes. It is water-soluble, and is lost when boiling vegetables and cooking fruit, and when there is prolonged dry heat in cooking.

RICHEST SOURCES
Yeast extract, cod's roe, offal (all kinds), avocado, wheat bran, cauliflower, cod, eggs, mushrooms, peanuts, sesame seeds, sunflower seeds, walnuts, wheatgerm and royal jelly of bees.

ESPECIALLY NEEDED BY
Those who are stressed or depressed, or who do not have enough fibre in their diets.

VITAMIN B6 (PYRIDOXINE)

Necessary in the metabolism of proteins and fats, is involved (with zinc) in the production of antibodies and red blood cells, prevents certain skin disorders, and a variety of nervous disorders. Involved in the formation of adrenalin and insulin, etc., for the production of RNA and DNA. It is water-soluble, and although fairly stable in cooking, can be lost if cooking water is discarded.

RICHEST SOURCES

Wheatgerm, liver (beef, calf, chicken), kidney, oily fish, soya beans, pulses, sunflower seeds, hazelnuts, walnuts (English), wheat bran, bananas, Brie cheese, Brussels sprouts, cabbage (red), carrots, dark green leafy vegetables, cauliflower, chestnuts, chicken, cod, sweetcorn, crab, cress, heart, kale, lentils, yeast extract, peanuts, pork, rabbit, rice bran.

ESPECIALLY NEEDED BY

Pregnant women, women of child-bearing age, vegetarians and vegans (most B6 is from animal sources), junk-food eaters, dieters, insomniacs and those under stress.

VITAMIN B12 (CYANOCOBALAMINE)

Essential for the functioning of all cells, in partnership with folic acid, helps to regenerate bone marrow and maintain nerve tissue, and plays an important role in the metabolism of protein, fat and carbohydrate. It is water-soluble, and is relatively stable in cooking, although up to 50 per cent can be lost if cooking water is discarded.

RICHEST SOURCES

Cod's roe, eel, heart (beef), herrings, kidney (beef), liver (beef, lamb), mackerel, oysters, sardines, cod, chicken liver, egg yolk, heart (lamb), trout. There are no vegetable sources of vitamin B12, so vegetarians and vegans may need to supplement.

ESPECIALLY NEEDED BY

Pregnant and lactating women, vegetarians and vegans (B12 is found *only* in animal foods), and the elderly.

FOLATE (FOLIC ACID)

Involved in cell growth, particularly red blood cells. Also important for proper function of the thymus gland. Important in pregnancy to prevent birth defects such as spina bifida. It is water-soluble, and can be lost easily in cooking by *over*cooking, by prolonged cooking and by reheating.

RICHEST SOURCES

Yeast extract, wheatgerm, egg yolk, liver and kidney (beef, lamb, pork), wheat bran, almonds, beet, broccoli, Brussels sprouts, peanuts, sesame seeds, wholegrain cereals, pulses.

ESPECIALLY NEEDED BY

Pregnant and lactating women, by women on the Pill or HRT, by children during times of rapid growth, by those who are stressed, and by the elderly.

VITAMIN C (ASCORBIC ACID)

Maintains collagen, connective tissue in the body, promotes healing of wounds, burns, injuries etc., helps to promote the integrity of the capillaries, and is essential for the specific metabolism of amino acids and iron. It increases resistance to infection. It is water-soluble, and a powerful antioxidant. C is easily lost in cooking, as it is affected by heat, light and oxygen; even cutting up vegetables can reduce their C levels. Cook whole vegetables if possible in minimum water for the minimum time.

RICHEST SOURCES

Blackcurrants (raw), grapefruit, guavas, lemons, spinach, kiwi fruit, orange, parsley, rocket, sweet and chilli peppers, cauliflower, watercress, blackcurrants (cooked), broccoli, Brussels sprouts, cabbage, dark green leafy vegetables, redcurrants, blackberries, gooseberries, mustard and cress, papaya, liver, kidney, potatoes, sprouted pulses, whole grains and seeds.

ESPECIALLY NEEDED BY

Infants, children, those suffering from stress, women during the menopause, and the elderly.

VITAMIN D (CALCIFEROL)

Needed for the absorption and use of calcium (bones and teeth). Might also be involved in maintaining the appetite. It is manufactured in exposed skin in sunlight. It is fat-soluble, and is fairly stable in cooking, although it is destroyed by light and oxygen.

RICHEST SOURCES

Cod liver oil, halibut liver oil, egg yolk, herring, sardine, eel, mackerel and other oily fish, oysters, tinned salmon, dairy products and liver.

ESPECIALLY NEEDED BY

Infants and adolescents, pregnant and lactating women, vegetarians, women going through the menopause, the elderly and those with dark skins living in more northerly countries.

VITAMIN E (TOCOPHERYLACETATE)

Important for protecting the body joints from oxidation and may also protect against heart disease. It is fat-soluble. Little is lost in home cooking, except when frying in fat, but it is unstable when frozen. Oils lose E content when exposed to light.

RICHEST SOURCES

Wheatgerm, alfalfa, cod liver oil, corn oil, rapeseed oil, rice bran, safflower oil, sesame seeds, sunflower oil, wheatgerm oil, almonds, buckwheat flour, hazelnuts, peanuts, pecans, walnuts, wheat bran, avocados, oats.

ESPECIALLY NEEDED BY

Everyone, because of its protective character.

III MINERALS

CALCIUM
Needed for bones, teeth and muscles. Adequate Vitamin D is necessary for its absorption.

SOURCES
Dairy products, dark green leafy vegetables, citrus fruits, canned fish with edible bones, pulses.

ESPECIALLY NEEDED BY
Pregnant and lactating women, children, junk-food eaters, dieters, women on the Pill or HRT or undergoing the menopause, insomniacs and the elderly.

CHROMIUM
Necessary for blood sugar control.

SOURCES
Whole grains, shellfish, nuts, mushrooms, wheatgerm.

ESPECIALLY NEEDED BY
Those under stress.

COPPER
Needed in the work of the enzymes.

SOURCES
Whole grains, pulses, shellfish, nuts, mushrooms, offal (especially foie gras), eggs, poultry, dark green leafy vegetables, chocolate.

IODINE
Needed for the normal functioning of the thyroid gland. A diet too rich in brassicas (the cabbage family) can interfere with iodine absorption.

SOURCES
Seafood, especially oily fish, seaweed, liver, pineapple, eggs, whole grains, dairy products.

ESPECIALLY NEEDED BY
Infants and pregnant women.

IRON

Needed by the blood to carry oxygen. Vitamin C helps its absorption. Too much tea or coffee depress iron absorption.

SOURCES

Liver, kidney, red meats, dried fruits, nuts, legumes, dark green leafy vegetables, sardines, prune juice, oysters, eggs, watercress, tomatoes.

ESPECIALLY NEEDED BY

Children, adolescents, women of child-bearing age, pregnant women, strict vegetarians.

MAGNESIUM

Part of chlorophyll, the green pigment in plants, needed for conversion of calories into energy. Tap water in hard-water areas supplies magnesium.

SOURCES

Dark green leafy vegetables, whole grains, nuts, legumes, seafood, chocolate, bananas.

ESPECIALLY NEEDED BY

Junk-food eaters, dieters, pregnant women, those under stress, those with high cholesterol.

MANGANESE

Needed in the work of the enzymes.

SOURCES

Wheatgerm, liver, kidney, green leafy vegetables, red meat, tea, whole grains, legumes, seeds, nuts, chocolate.

ESPECIALLY NEEDED BY

Pregnant women, or women undergoing the menopause.

PHOSPHORUS

Needed for the teeth and bones, and release of energy.

SOURCES

Meats, fish, poultry, eggs, dairy products, grains, fruit and vegetables.

ESPECIALLY NEEDED BY

Those under stress.

POTASSIUM

Needed for heart, muscles and maintenance of normal blood glucose levels.

SOURCES

Lean meats, pulses, wheatgerm, whole grains, potatoes, bananas, nuts, orange juice, avocados, apricots.

ESPECIALLY NEEDED BY

Those under stress.

SELENIUM

Needed to work with the detoxifier glutathione as a co-factor and antioxidant.

SOURCES

Liver, kidney, meats, seafood, dairy products, whole grains, pineapples.

ZINC

Needed for bones and enzymes.

SOURCES

Oysters, herring, milk, meat, egg yolks, corn, beets, peas, almonds, pulses.

ESPECIALLY NEEDED BY

Pregnant and lactating women, adolescents, children experiencing growth spurts, junk-food eaters, dieters, strict vegetarians, those suffering stress, women during the menopause, those physically exerting themselves, the elderly.

IV ORGANIC FOOD

Because I am so enthusiastic about organic food, I asked representatives of the two principal organic organisations to describe and explain their work.

THE SOIL ASSOCIATION

FRANCIS BLAKE, CERTIFICATION DIRECTOR

'The health of soil, plant, animal and man is one and indivisible.' So said the founder of the Soil Association, Lady Eve Balfour, in her book, The Living Soil, that was the catalyst for the formation of the organisation back in 1946. Today, these far-sighted words ring as true as ever and, after half a century of decline (or worse) in our health and that of the environment, they have taken on an urgency that we ignore at our peril.

The Soil Association is a registered charity (no. 206862), founded to research, develop and promote these close and direct inter-relationships between the health of soils, plants, animals, people and the wider environment. It considers that organic agriculture and sustainable resource use provide the most practical implementation of this founding principle. It works to ensure that these practices are respected in the way both farming and forestry are conducted and also in how agricultural, environmental and health policy is formulated.

It researches both the problems that the world is facing today in these areas, and also promotes practical solutions to these problems – ways to strengthen the linkages and create more balanced farming systems, more healthy food and more sustainable use of resources. It runs educational and promotional campaigns and produces and sells a range of its own and other publications. It also educates policy makers towards more sensitive and integrated policies. Last, but not least, it supports and represents organic producers and those wishing to convert to organic production.

There is still much to achieve, though, and Britain has only a very small proportion of its agricultural land farmed organically (Austria, for example, has 8 per cent). One of the main differences is the level of support for organic agriculture provided by governments. Britain is at the bottom of this league table, but direct support is only one aspect. Also important is investment in research and advice. Here the UK also lags behind. The challenge for our Government is now clear . . .

Eat organic and enjoy safe, healthy, nutritious food produced in a way that does not damage the soil, plants, animals or people.

THE HENRY DOUBLEDAY RESEARCH ASSOCIATION

ALAN GEAR, CHIEF EXECUTIVE,

AND JACKIE GEAR, EXECUTIVE DIRECTOR

In the 1970s it was obvious that scientific progress alone was not going to guarantee the welfare and long-term future of our planet. We felt that we ought to put our scientific qualifications to better use. So we resigned from thriving careers to work for a little-known charity with a strange name – 'The Henry Doubleday Research Association'. Named after a Quaker smallholder, and run by a wise and knowledgeable man called Lawrence Hills, it was an experimenting body, with gardening and scientific members, interested in environmentally friendly, sustainable organic gardening and farming. From humble beginnings HDRA is now internationally respected, and is the largest organic organisation in Europe.

Organic food is one of the few foods you can trust. Because the organic symbol is backed up by legislation, if you see an organic symbol on a food product, you know exactly what you are getting. Organic food also tastes better. The 'artificial' inorganic fertilisers favoured by modern farmers generally result in a greater water uptake by the crop. More water means less flavour. Because organic livestock are fed on naturally complex organic nutrients, both as rich herbal pastures, silage and concentrates, organic meat tastes stronger. I defy anyone not to be able to tell the difference between a typical frozen, factory-farmed, supermarket chicken and a free-range organic bird. As for eggs, anyone who cannot distinguish a free-range organic egg from its factory-farmed equivalent does not deserve to be cooking.

Organic food not only tastes better and richer, it is better for you. It contains more vitamins and minerals and because it is produced without chemicals it does not carry the risk that a continuous intake of dozens of pesticides poses to health.

There have been several surveys of the general public, to find out their attitudes towards organic food, and they have shown conclusively that the majority of people would buy organic food if it were the same price as that produced conventionally. A supermarket chain that deliberately kept prices of its organic products the same as its other lines found this was indeed the case. So why has the Government not been more supportive of organic farming?

At the time of writing, organic farmers do not receive any special financial incentive, other than when converting from non-organic to organic. Last year the total budget for encouraging organic farming in the UK was set by the Ministry of Agriculture at a mere £1 million. Compare this with the £1 million cash that was paid in subsidies to each of five conventional farmers. This is utter madness!

We know that organic gardening and farming works. It is sensible and it is sustainable. It may cost more to buy organic food at present, but that is a result of flawed EC subsidies. Organic food is not intrinsically more expensive to produce. In any case, if you cannot buy it, you can always grow your own!

INDEX